Wonderful WORLD

SECOND EDITION

GRAMMAR BOOK

Australia • Brazil • Mexico • Singapore • United Kingdom • United States

Contents

		Page
Unit 0	Plurals; Articles; Demonstratives	4
Unit 1		
Lesson 1	Be	10
Lesson 2	Possessive adjectives	13
Lesson 3	Possessive 's	15
Unit 2		
Lesson 1	Have got	17
Lesson 2	There is, There are	20
Review: Units 1 – 2		24
Unit 3		
Lesson 1	Present simple affirmative	27
Lesson 2	Present simple negative and questions	30
Lesson 3	Adverbs of frequency	33
Unit 4		
Lesson 1	Question words	36
Lesson 2	Can	39
Review: Units 3 – 4		42
Unit 5		
Lesson 1	Imperative; Object pronouns; Let's	45
Lesson 2	Countable and uncountable nouns	48
Lesson 3	Some, any	51
Unit 6		
Lesson 1	Much, many	54
Lesson 2	A lot of, lots of, a few, a little	56
Review: Units 5 – 6		59
Unit 7		
Lesson 1	Present continuous affirmative	62
Lesson 2	Present continuous negative and questions	65
Lesson 3	Present continuous (to express the future)	68
Unit 8		
Lesson 1	Present simple and present continuous	71
Lesson 2	Must	74
Review: Units 7 – 8		77
Unit 9		
Lesson 1	Past simple: Be	80
Lesson 2	Past simple affirmative: Regular verbs	83
Lesson 3	Past simple affirmative: Irregular verbs	86
Unit 10		
Lesson 1	Past simple negative and questions: Regular and irregular verbs	89
Lesson 2	Question words with the past simple	92
Review: Units 9 – 10		94
Unit 11		
Lesson 1	Comparatives; as … as	97
Lesson 2	Superlatives	100
Lesson 3	Comparatives and superlatives	103
Unit 12		
Lesson 1	Be going to	106
Lesson 2	Future simple	109
Review: Units 11 – 12		112
Irregular verbs		115

0 Introduction

1 Read.

Carlos loves tomatoes!

Plurals

We usually add –**s** to a noun to make it plural.
pen   pen**s**
hut   hut**s**
book   book**s**

We add –**es** to nouns that end in –**s**, –**ss**, –**sh**, –**ch** and –**x**.
box   box**es**
beach   beach**es**
watch   watch**es**

When a word ends in a consonant + –**y**, we take off the –**y** and add –**ies**.
family   famil**ies**
lady   lad**ies**
party   part**ies**

When a word ends in a vowel + –**y**, we just add –**s**. Sometimes, both –**s** and –**es** are possible.
day   day**s**
boy   boy**s**
toy   toy**s**

We usually add –**s** to nouns that end in –**o**, but we sometimes add –**es**. Sometimes, both –**s** and –**es** are possible.
photo   photo**s**
tomato   tomato**es**
potato   potato**es**
volcano   volcan**o** or volcano**es**

When a noun ends in –**f**, or –**fe**, we usually take off the –**f** or –**fe** and add –**ves**. We just add –**s** to the words **giraffe** and **roof**. Sometimes, both forms are possible.
wife   wi**ves**
knife   kni**ves**
life   li**ves**
giraffe   giraffe**s**
roof   roof**s**
scarf   scarf**s** or scar**ves**

Remember!

Some nouns are irregular and they do not follow these rules.

child	**children**	mouse	**mice**
fish	**fish**	sheep	**sheep**
foot	**feet**	tooth	**teeth**
man	**men**	woman	**women**

2 Write the plural of these words.

box   child   family   ~~fish~~   giraffe   mouse   pencil   potato   toy

1 two __fish__

2 twelve _____

3 seven _____

4 five _____

5 six _____

6 fourteen _____

7 two _____

8 three _____

9 two _____

3 Write the plurals.

baby   beach   ~~bicycles~~   boat   city   glass   sheep   sky   tooth   tree   watch   woman

–s	–es	–ies	Irregular
bicycles			

4 Say it! Talk about things you've got. Use plural nouns.

I've got two watches.

I've got two boxes of crayons.

5 Read.

There's a hot-air balloon in the sky.

Articles

We use **a** and **an** (indefinite articles) with singular nouns.
a snake
an orange

We use **a** before nouns that begin with a consonant (b, c, d, f, g, h, j, k, l, m, n, p, q, r, s, t, v, w, x, y, z).
a boat
a tree

We use **an** before nouns that begin with a vowel (a, e, i, o, u).
an elephant
an island

Sometimes there is an adjective before the noun. We use **a** when the adjective begins with a consonant.
We use **an** when the adjective begins with a vowel.
a new album
an amazing game

We use **a** or **an** to talk about one person, animal or thing in general.
There is *a* spider in the kitchen.
He's got *a* new bag.

We use **the** instead of **a/an** to talk about a specific person, animal or thing, or to talk about it, or them, again.
There's *a* big tree in our garden. *The* tree has big red flowers in spring.
The children next door go to my school.

We also use **the** to talk about something which is unique, for example *the sky, the moon, the sun*.
The sun is up in *the* sky.

The can be used with plural nouns.
I need books and paper. *The* books are for my English class. The paper is for my art class.

Remember!

Be careful with words that begin with **h** or **u**! When the word begins with a consonant sound, we use **a**. When the word begins with a vowel sound, we use **an**.
a house, **an** hour, **a** uniform, **an** uncle

6 Write *a* or *an*.

1 _an_ eye
2 _____ green apple
3 _____ box
4 _____ door
5 _____ ear
6 _____ hour
7 _____ egg
8 _____ exciting hobby
9 _____ house

7 Write *a*, *an* or *the*.

1 Look! There's __a__ whale in __the__ sea.
2 This isn't _____ teddy bear. It's _____ doll.
3 There's _____ black desk in my bedroom. On _____ desk, there's _____ fish tank.
4 Look! There's _____ big bird in _____ sky.
5 _____ moon looks so beautiful tonight. Let's look at it with _____ binoculars.
6 I've got _____ pet cat. He likes to sleep on _____ floor in my bedroom.

8 Say it! Talk about the picture. Use *a, an, the* and these suggestions to help you.

- bed
- book
- cat
- chair
- clock
- desk
- football
- helicopter
- school bag
- sky
- sun
- teddy bear

He's got a school bag. The school bag is big.

9 Read.

This cat is friendly. **That cat is angry.**

Demonstratives

We use demonstratives to show that someone or something is near us (**this**, **these**) or further away (**that**, **those**).

Singular	Plural
this	these
that	those

This book is for you. *That* one over there is for your sister.
I like *these* dolls here. *Those* dolls on the shelf over there are for babies!

10 Circle the correct words.

1 **That** / **This** car across the street is very cool.
2 **That** / **This** box in my hands is a present for you.
3 I really like **that** / **those** flowers.
4 **These** / **This** are my books. **Those** / **That** over there are my sister's books.
5 I like **this** / **these** robot. I want it for my birthday.
6 **That** / **Those** fish looks funny.

11 Complete the sentences with *this, that, these* or *those*.

1. These are my shoes.
2. _____ is my phone.
3. _____ bird is beautiful.
4. _____ is your ruler.
5. _____ flowers are very nice.
6. _____ are my chocolates!

12 Say it! Talk about things in your classroom. Use *this, that, these, those* and these suggestions to help you.

- ruler
- books
- school bag
- pencil
- desks
- pens
- clock
- students

These books are mine.

That's Mario's school bag.

Lesson 1

1 Read.

Be

We use **be** with subject pronouns (I, you, he, etc.) or with other nouns.
He **is** hungry.
Sharks **are** grey.

We use **be** to talk about someone's job, nationality, relationship, or his or her name.
He **is** a scientist.   We **are** sisters.
They **are** English.   I **am** Carlos.

We also use **be** to describe people or things.
Robbie **is** young.
The hut **is** old.

We use the short form in everyday English.
Hi, **I'm** Ana.

Remember!

In English, there is no difference between **you** singular and **you** plural.

Affirmative	Negative	Question	Short answers	
I'm (I am)	I'm not (I am not)	Am I …?	Yes, I am.	No, I'm not.
you're (you are)	you aren't (you are not)	Are you …?	Yes, you are.	No, you aren't.
he's (he is)	he isn't (he is not)	Is he …?	Yes, he is.	No, he isn't.
she's (she is)	she isn't (she is not)	Is she …?	Yes, she is.	No, she isn't.
it's (it is)	it isn't (it is not)	Is it …?	Yes, it is.	No, it isn't.
we're (we are)	we aren't (we are not)	Are we …?	Yes, we are.	No, we aren't.
you're (you are)	you aren't (you are not)	Are you …?	Yes, you are.	No, you aren't.
they're (they are)	they aren't (they are not)	Are they …?	Yes, they are.	No, they aren't.

2 Write the sentences again with the short form of *be*.

1. You are very tall.   You're very tall.
2. He is clever.   _____
3. We are not on holiday.   _____
4. I am in the garden.   _____
5. They are not cousins.   _____
6. She is not happy.   _____
7. They are very loud.   _____
8. It is not a good idea.   _____

3 Look at the picture and complete the sentences with the correct form of *be*.

1. The children aren't/are not at school.
2. It _____ a beautiful day.
3. It _____ cold.
4. They _____ at the beach.
5. The water _____ warm.
6. It _____ winter.
7. They _____ happy.
8. Holidays _____ cool!

4 Complete the sentences about you with the correct form of *be*.

1. I 'm/'m not / am/am not from Egypt.
2. I _____ crazy about science.
3. My dad _____ a scientist.
4. My mum _____ nice.
5. My friends and I _____ at school now.
6. My cousins _____ funny.
7. I _____ nine years old.
8. My house _____ new.

11

5 Look at the picture and answer the questions.

1 Is it a rainy day? <u>No, it isn't.</u>
2 Are the girls happy? _____
3 Is the house small? _____
4 Are the cats white? _____
5 Is the dog big? _____
6 Is the door black? _____
7 Is the boy tall? _____
8 Is the car very old? _____

6 Complete the questions with *am, are* or *is*. Then complete the short answers.

1 <u>Is</u> Clara your new friend?
   Yes, <u>she is</u>.
2 _____ you crazy about school?
   No, _____.
3 _____ the cats in the garden?
   Yes, _____.
4 _____ your brother young?
   No, _____.
5 _____ your cats black?
   Yes, _____.
6 _____ I strong?
   Yes, _____.
7 _____ you and Baldo cousins?
   No, _____.
8 _____ you 12 years old?
   No, _____.

7 Circle the correct words.

1 **Is /(Are)** we at the beach?
2 My cousin **is / are** cool.
3 Sharks **isn't / aren't** red.
4 **Is / Are** they sisters?
5 Uncle Joe **isn't / aren't** in the house.
6 I **am / are** in the water.
7 You **isn't / aren't** short.
8 **Is / Are** the baby happy?

8 Say it! Ask and answer the questions with your partner.

Are you at the beach now?

No, I'm not.

- Is your school new?
- Is your best friend tall?
- Is your uncle a teacher?
- Is your classroom big?
- Are your cousins clever?
- Is your birthday in April?
- Are you 12 years old?

12 UNIT 1

Lesson 2

1 Read.

My cousin is cool!

Possessive adjectives

Possessive adjectives show that something belongs to someone or something. They go before the noun.

My little sister is beautiful. **Her** hair is long.
The house is small. **Its** door is green.

Subject pronouns	Possessive adjectives
I	my
you	your
he	his
she	her
it	its
we	our
you	your
they	their

Remember !

Be careful with these words:
it's (it is) and **its**.
you're (you are) and **your**.
he's (he is) and **his**.

2 Complete the sentences with possessive adjectives.

1 This house is amazing! Is it ___your___ house? (you)
2 Amy is _____ sister. (I)
3 Elisabeth and I are cousins. _____ mothers are sisters. (we)
4 Is Mr Lee _____ teacher? (she)
5 It's very warm in _____ house. (we)
6 Dad is 38 years old. _____ name is Mark. (he)
7 Is _____ father a scientist? (they)
8 The cat is white. _____ eyes are green. (it)

13

3 Look at the pictures and complete the sentences with these possessive adjectives.

her   its   ~~my~~   our   their   your

1. This is me. I'm with __my__ grandma.
2. Dad and I are with _____ dog, Moose.
3. Here's Mum. It's _____ birthday.
4. Look at you! _____ hair is very short!
5. Look at my fish. _____ names are Sharky and Nemo.
6. Here's my rabbit. _____ ears are big!

4 Match.

1. The girls are sisters.
2. I'm on holiday with Mum and Dad.
3. Grandma is very beautiful.
4. Rick is my best friend.
5. I'm at school.

a. His birthday is in August.
b. My classroom is small.
c. Her eyes are dark green.
d. Our hotel is on the beach.
e. Their names are Cindy and Sally.

5 Circle the correct words.

1. The girls are happy. **Its / Their** dolls are beautiful.
2. This is my pet rabbit. **Their / Its** ears are very long.
3. Mr Shaw is next to **his / its** car.
4. Father penguins keep **its / their** eggs warm.
5. Lucy is crazy about **her / its** horse.
6. Wang and I are brothers. **Our / Their** eyes are brown.
7. I'm nine years old today! It's **her / my** birthday.
8. You're clever. **Its / Your** idea is cool!

6 Say it! Tell your partner about your family. Use possessive adjectives to talk about their names, jobs and birthdays.

> My uncle is a teacher. His name is Tim and his birthday is in June.

14   UNIT 1

Lesson 3

1 Read.

It's Grandma's birthday.

Possessive 's

We use **'s** to show that something belongs to someone or something.
This is Natalia's book.

We add **'s** to singular nouns.
This is the penguin's egg.

When the noun is plural, we add an apostrophe after the **–s**.
This is the boys' house.

But when the noun has an irregular plural, we add **'s**.
The children's hair is dark.
The women's daughters are clever.

2 Complete the sentences with the possessive *'s* ('s or '). Use the words in brackets.

1 The ___girl's___ idea is great! (girl)
2 _____ lemonade is on the table. (Grandma)
3 The _____ dog is cool. (twins)
4 Your _____ cat is hungry. (cousins)
5 My _____ job is amazing. (uncle)
6 The _____ grandad is in the water. (children)
7 Is the _____ mum in the hut? (boys)
8 The _____ sister is tall. (babies)

3 Look at the pictures and circle the correct words.

1 Jack is the **girl's /(girls')** father.

2 The **boy's / boys'** hands are cold.

3 The **chimp's / chimps'** arms are long.

4 The **penguin's / penguins'** chick is beautiful.

5 The **women's / woman's** husbands are tall.

6 The **bird's / birds'** feet are red.

4 Choose the correct answers.

1 Is that your _____ brother?
  a grandmas'   b) grandma's
2 My _____ house is near the sea.
  a parent's   b parents'
3 _____ cousins are in Africa.
  a Mum's   b Mums'
4 The two _____ husbands are friends.
  a women's   b woman's
5 _____ friend is cool.
  a Dad's   b Dads'
6 What's the _____ name?
  a doctor's   b doctors'
7 My _____ names are Carla, Bea and Marta.
  a sister's   b sisters'
8 The _____ birthday is in April.
  a man's   b men's

5 Say it! Ask and answer questions with your partner about you, your family, your friends and your teachers.

What's your ...'s name?

Her/His name is ...

- Is your ...'s house big?
- When is your ...'s birthday?
- What's your ...'s favourite colour?
- What's your ...'s favourite lesson?
- What's your ...'s favourite game?
- What's your friend's name?
- What's your pet's name?

Lesson 1

2

1 Read.

He's got a new video game.

Have got

We use **have got** to show that something belongs to someone or something.
He**'s got** a new laptop.

We use **have got** to describe someone or something.
His new laptop **has got** many games.

Affirmative	Negative
I've got (I have got) you've got (you have got) he's got (he has got) she's got (she has got) it's got (it has got) we've got (we have got) you've got (you have got) they've got (they have got)	I haven't got (I have not got) you haven't got (you have not got) he hasn't got (he has not got) she hasn't got (she has not got) it hasn't got (it has not got) we haven't got (we have not got) you haven't got (you have not got) they haven't got (they have not got)

Question	Short answers	
Have I got ...?	Yes, I have.	No, I haven't.
Have you got ...?	Yes, you have.	No, you haven't.
Has he got ...?	Yes, he has.	No, he hasn't.
Has she got ...?	Yes, she has.	No, she hasn't.
Has it got ...?	Yes, it has.	No, it hasn't.
Have we got ...?	Yes, we have.	No, we haven't.
Have you got ...?	Yes, you have.	No, you haven't.
Have they got ...?	Yes, they have.	No, they haven't.

Remember!

Be careful with **its** (possessive adjective) and **it's** (it has) got.

2 **Complete the sentences with the short form of *have got*.**

1 She ___'s got___ a board game.
2 I _____ a new skateboard. It's cool!
3 You _____ a strange message. It's a mystery!
4 They _____ a real lizard.
5 We _____ lots of video games.
6 The dog is happy. It _____ a ball.

3 **Complete the sentences with the negative form of *have got*.**

1 Mum and I ___haven't got___ a map with us.
2 I _____ a present for Mae.
3 My cousin Tobias _____ a real robot.
4 The city _____ lots of museums.
5 You _____ a new toy.
6 Aunt Lila and Uncle Marco _____ new mobile phones.

4 **Complete the questions using *have got* and the words in brackets. Then complete the short answers.**

1 ___Have Liz and Pete got___ a red pen? (Liz and Pete)
   No, ___they haven't___ .
2 _____ a laptop? (you)
   No, _____ .
3 _____ a house in Spain? (she)
   Yes, _____ .
4 _____ a fast bike? (Jason)
   Yes, _____ .
5 _____ the pieces of the puzzle? (we)
   No, _____ .
6 _____ a pet? (I)
   Yes, _____ .

5 **Circle the correct words.**

1 Josh **haven't** / **(hasn't)** got a picture of a dragon in his room.
2 **Have** / **Has** they got a new puzzle?
3 Sammy **have** / **has** got a house near the sea.
4 **Have** / **Has** you got a message on your mobile phone?
5 The children **have** / **has** got a teddy bear.
6 **Have** / **Has** Uncle Harry got a camera?
7 We **haven't** / **hasn't** got any boots.
8 **Have** / **Has** I got an ant in my hair?

6 Look at the pictures. Write the questions and answer them.

1 has / got / bicycle / ? / he / a
   Has he got a bicycle?
   Yes, he has.

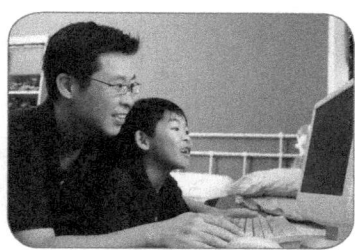

4 ? / the / laptop / got / has / a / father
   _____
   _____

2 she / game / ? / has / got / video / a
   _____
   _____

5 has / homework / she / got / ?
   _____
   _____

3 ? / they / laptops / got / have
   _____
   _____

6 got / have / they / ? / sandwiches
   _____
   _____

7 Say it! Ask and answer questions with your partner about what you have and haven't got. Use these suggestions to help you.

   Have you got a kite?   Yes, I have.

- bike
- brother
- cat

- video games
- dog
- garden

- laptop
- phone
- sister

19

Lesson 2

1 Read.

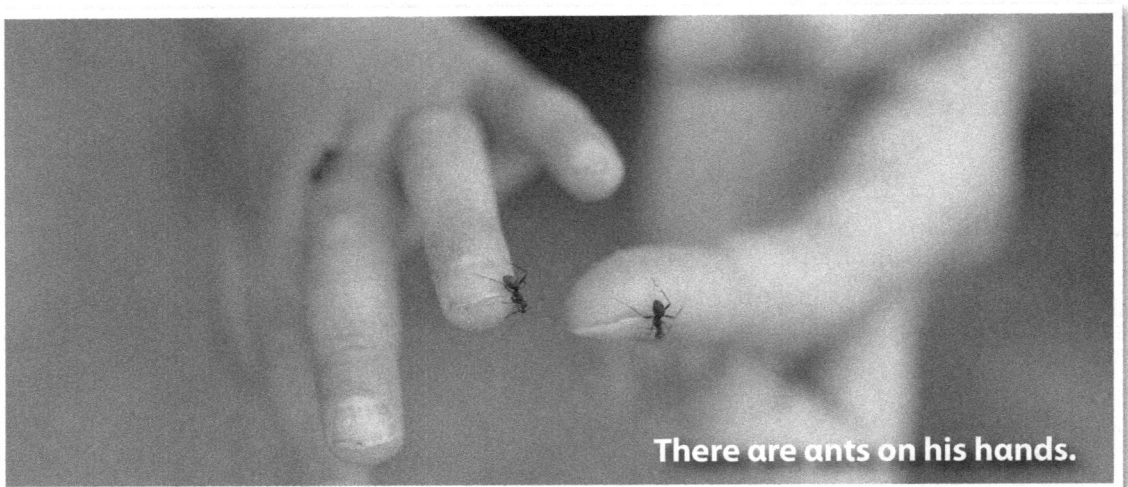

There are ants on his hands.

There is, There are

We use **there is** and **there are** to talk or ask about what exists when we are describing something in the present.
There are two mobile phones on the table.
Is there a snake in the bedroom?

We use **there is** and **there are** to describe situations and places.
There is a lizard in the garden.
There aren't any toys in the box.

Affirmative	Negative	Question	Short answers	
There's (There is) There are	There isn't (There is not) There aren't (There are not)	Is there ...? Are there ...?	Yes, there is. Yes, there are.	No, there isn't. No, there aren't.

Prepositions of place

We use **prepositions of place** to show where someone or something is.

behind
The ball is **behind** the box.

near
The ball is **near** the box.

between
The ball is **between** the boxes.

next to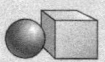
The ball is **next to** the box.

in
The ball is **in** the box.

on
The ball is **on** the box.

in front of
The ball is **in front of** the box.

under
The ball is **under** the box.

at the top/bottom **at** school/work/home	**in** hospital **in** bed **in** the middle	**on** the left/right **on** the plane/train/bus

2 Complete the sentences with *There is, There are, There isn't* or *There aren't*.

1. _There aren't_ any koalas in Europe. ✗
2. _____ some good puzzles in the toy shop. ✓
3. _____ a young girl on the beach. ✓
4. _____ any lizards in the sea. ✗
5. _____ a picture of a fish in my book. ✓
6. _____ a phone on the desk. ✗

3 Look at the pictures and answer the questions.

1. Is there a map in the boy's hand?
   Yes, there is.

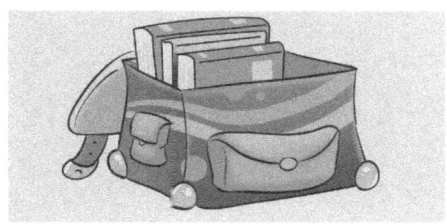

2. Are there any books in the bag?
   _____

3. Is there a robot in the shop window?
   _____

4. Are there any boots under the bed?
   _____

5. Is there a board game on the desk?
   _____

6. Is there an astronaut on the moon?
   _____

4 Complete the questions and short answers.

1 <u>Are there</u> any scary animals in the video game?
No, <u>there aren't</u>.

2 _____ a new message on your phone?
Yes, _____ .

3 _____ any board games at school?
No, _____ .

4 _____ a toy robot near the window?
Yes, _____ .

5 _____ any watches in the shop?
Yes, _____ .

6 _____ a guitar in your bedroom?
No, _____ .

5 Look at the pictures and complete the sentences with these words.

| behind between in in front of ~~on~~ under |

1 The globe is ___on___ the box.

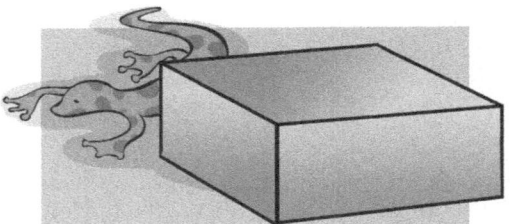

4 The lizard is _____ the box.

2 The shoes are _____ the box.

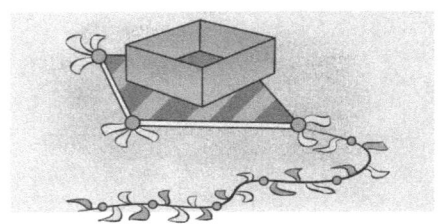

5 The kite is _____ the box.

3 The teddy bear is _____ the box.

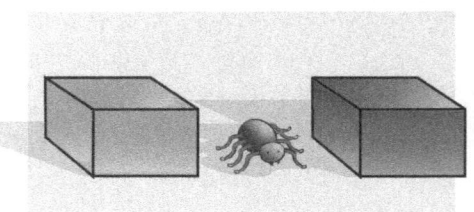

6 The spider is _____ the boxes.

6 Look at the picture and answer the questions.

1 Is there a skateboard on the table?
   <u>No, there isn't.</u>

2 Is there a bike under the window?
   _____

3 Are there two mobile phones behind the laptop?
   _____

4 Is there a clock between the lizard and the picture?
   _____

5 Are there any eggs in the box?
   _____

6 Is there a picture next to the door?
   _____

7 Say it! Tell your partner about your bedroom. Say what there is and isn't in your bedroom. Use prepositions of place to describe where things are in the room.

> My bedroom is small, but it's got a big window. There is a desk next to the window ...

Review

1 Complete the sentences with *be*.

1 The camera __is__ new. ✓
2 You _____ happy today. ✗
3 The astronaut _____ very tall. ✓
4 We _____ hungry. ✗
5 Mum and Dad _____ at the museum. ✗
6 I _____ crazy about computer games. ✗
7 The skateboard _____ amazing! ✓
8 It _____ warm today. ✗

2 Complete the sentences with possessive adjectives.

1 I've got a laptop. __My__ laptop is cool!
2 That's my friend Steven. _____ birthday is today.
3 You've got a new phone! _____ mobile phone is great.
4 We've got a rabbit. _____ rabbit is hungry.
5 There is a spider on the floor! _____ legs are very long.
6 Keyu and Lee have got a kite. _____ kite is in the sky!

3 Match.

1 Is the lizard ugly?   a No, you aren't.
2 Are the chicks cold?   b Yes, he is.
3 Am I funny?   c Yes, she is.
4 Is Mike a good swimmer?   d No, I'm not.
5 Are you a pupil?   e Yes, it is.
6 Is she French?   f Yes, they are.

4 Look at the pictures and complete the sentences with prepositions of place.

1 The chair is __in front of__ the umbrella.
2 The orange is _____ the apple.
3 The cat is _____ the chair.
4 The boy is _____ the tree.
5 The cat is _____ the box.
6 The umbrella is _____ the chairs.

5 Look at the pictures and complete the sentences using the possessive 's.

| boy | boys | children | girl | girls | ~~twins~~ |

1 The ___twins'___ presents are big.   4 The _____ bike is new.

2 The _____ teacher is short.   5 The _____ skateboard is fast.

3 The _____ boots are old.   6 The _____ hats are funny.

6 Complete the questions using *have got* and the words in brackets. Then complete the short answers.

1 ___Has the penguin got___ big feet? (the penguin)
No, ___it hasn't___ .

2 _____ a map? (we)
Yes, _____ .

3 _____ a photo of a penguin? (Uncle Tony)
No, _____ .

4 _____ a strange pet? (Rick and Emily)
Yes, _____ .

5 _____ an exciting job? (you)
Yes, _____ .

6 _____ long hair? (Carla)
No, _____ .

7 Complete the sentences with *have got*.

1 I __'ve/have got__ a great idea! ✓
2 Sandy _____ lots of emails. ✗
3 We _____ a grey cat. ✓
4 Jason _____ dark eyes. ✓
5 You _____ a lot of homework today. ✗
6 My grandparents _____ a very beautiful garden. ✓

8 Circle the correct words.

1 **There isn't / There aren't** a lot of houses on the beach.
2 **There are / There is** three presents in Kate's room.
3 **Is there / Are there** two teddy bears on the bed?
4 **There aren't / There isn't** a map of Africa in the classroom.
5 **There is / There are** a laptop on the desk.
6 **Is there / Are there** a small bottle of water in your bag?

WRITING PROJECT

9 Look at a project about sharks. Circle the correct words.

Sharks

Sharks (1) **has got / have got** a bad name. People think they are scary, but most sharks (2) **is not / are not** dangerous.

Sharks (3) **is / are** a kind of fish.

(4) **There is / There are** about 400 kinds of sharks around the world. The smallest shark, the dwarf lanternshark, is 17 centimetres long. The largest, the whale shark, (5) **is / are** 12 metres long.

The Caribbean reef shark can grow to about 3 metres. It (6) **has got / have got** big eyes, but its teeth (7) **is not / are not** very big. It lives close to coral reefs. (8) **It's / Its** favourite food is fish.

whale shark

10 Now it's your turn to do a project about an animal. Find or draw a picture of the animal and write about it.

Lesson 1

3

1 Read.

Marcela likes maths. She studies maths every day.

Present simple affirmative

We use the **present simple** to talk about
- general truths.
  *It **snows** in winter.*
- things that we do regularly.
  *On Saturdays we **go** to the beach.*
- permanent situations.
  *My grandparents **live** in Spain.*

We form the affirmative of the third person singular (he, she, it) by adding **–s** to the verb.
like   like**s**
eat   eat**s**
give   give**s**

We form the affirmative of the third person singular of verbs that end in **–ss**, **–sh**, **–ch**, **–x** and **–o**, by adding **–es**.
miss   miss**es**   fix   fix**es**
wash   wash**es**   do   do**es**
touch touch**es**

When a verb ends in a consonant + **–y**, we take off the **–y** and add **–ies** to form the affirmative of the third person singular.
study   stud**ies**   carry   carr**ies**

When a verb ends in a vowel + **–y**, we just add **–s** to form the affirmative of the third person singular.
play   play**s**   stay   stay**s**

Time expressions
The following time expressions go at the beginning or at the end of a sentence: **every day/night/week/month/year**, **at the weekend**, **in the morning/afternoon/evening**, **on Thursdays/Saturdays**, etc.
*My cousin cleans his room **every Saturday**.*
***On Wednesdays** we go to my aunt's house.*

Affirmative
I sing
you sing
he sings
she sings
it sings
we sing
you sing
they sing

2 **Complete the table.**

Verb	I/you/we/they	he/she/it
carry	carry	carries
fix		
give		
go		
like		
stay		
touch		
wash		

3 **Choose the correct answers.**

1 Paul and Hannah _____ in a museum.
   ⓐ work   b works

2 Kate _____ lots of fish.
   a eat   b eats

3 We _____ our pet rabbit at home.
   a keep   b keeps

4 Every year, you _____ me a nice present on my birthday.
   a gives   b give

5 I _____ music in my bedroom.
   a plays   b play

6 They _____ their phones all the time.
   a use   b uses

4 **Complete the sentences with the present simple. Use the verbs in brackets.**

1 In winter it _____snows_____ in Canada. (snow)
2 Maren _____ TV in the evening. (watch)
3 Our cousins _____ with us every summer. (stay)
4 Every morning, Pat _____ his books to school. (carry)
5 Aunt Liz _____ in a museum. (work)
6 I _____ English. It's my favourite subject. (like)
7 We _____ a calculator for our maths homework. (use)
8 My dad _____ his car every weekend. (wash)

5 Write sentences with the present simple.

1 she / like / art
   She likes art.

2 on Fridays / Mark / go / to the park
   _____

3 Maria / tidy / her room at the weekend
   _____

4 I / do / my homework in my bedroom
   _____

5 Natalie / know / the correct answer
   _____

6 we / brush / our teeth every morning and every evening
   _____

6 Complete the text with the present simple. Use these words.

| brush   come   go   have   love   ~~play~~   sit   watch |

On Friday morning, Sofia and I (1) __play__ computer games. Then we walk to the park. Sofia (2) _____ the park.

In the afternoon, we (3) _____ TV in my bedroom. Sofia (4) _____ on my bed with Felix, my cat. In the evening, Sofia and I (5) _____ our teeth and we (6) _____ to bed.

On Saturday, Sofia's mum (7) _____ to our house to get her.

We (8) _____ lots of fun. Sofia is cool!

Sofia and I

7 Say it! Tell your partner what you do every week. Use these suggestions to help you.

- at the weekend
- every day
- in the morning
- in the afternoon
- in the evening
- on Sundays, Mondays, etc.

Every day, I go to school.

Lesson 2

1 Read.

They don't wear a uniform.
Do you wear a uniform?

Present simple negative and questions

In the negative form, we use **do** or **does**, the word **not** and the infinitive of the main verb without **to** (bare infinitive).
I **don't like** history.
Mark **doesn't wash** his bike every week.

In the question form, we use **do** or **does** and the bare infinitive.
Do you **study** English?
Does she **carry** her books to school?

In short answers, we only use **do** or **does**. We don't use the main verb.
Does she like my skateboard?
Yes, she **does**.
Do they have science lessons at school?
Yes, they **do**.

Negative	Question	Short answers	
I don't play (I do not play)	Do I play?	Yes, I do.	No, I don't.
you don't play (you do not play)	Do you play?	Yes, you do.	No, you don't.
he doesn't play (he does not play)	Does he play?	Yes, he does.	No, he doesn't.
she doesn't play (she does not play)	Does she play?	Yes, she does.	No, she doesn't.
it doesn't play (it does not play)	Does it play?	Yes, it does.	No, it doesn't.
we don't play (we do not play)	Do we play?	Yes, we do.	No, we don't.
you don't play (you do not play)	Do you play?	Yes, you do.	No, you don't.
they don't play (they do not play)	Do they play?	Yes, they do.	No, they don't.

2 Complete the sentences with the negative form of the present simple. Use the verbs in brackets.

1 Max ____doesn't eat____ pasta at school. (eat)
2 I _____ my teeth in the afternoon. (brush)
3 They _____ fun in the geography lesson. (have)
4 We _____ in the library. (play)
5 Sandy _____ her homework at the weekend. (do)
6 You _____ in front of the bookcase. (sit)
7 Our teacher _____ a laptop. (use)
8 We _____ Japanese food. (eat)

3 Complete the questions with *do* or *does*. Then complete the short answers.

1 ____Does____ she have fun at school?
No, __she doesn't__ .

2 _____ Tara eat burgers?
Yes, _____ .

3 _____ they get up at ten o'clock on Saturdays?
Yes, _____ .

4 _____ you like eggs for breakfast?
No, _____ .

5 _____ he go to the canteen for lunch?
No, _____ .

6 _____ we sing in the music lesson?
Yes, _____ .

7 _____ Mrs Gomez use the globe in the geography lesson?
Yes, _____ .

8 _____ they carry their laptops to school?
No, _____ .

4 Write questions with these words. Then answer the questions so they are true for you.

1 you / wear / a uniform to school
   Do you wear a uniform to school?
   Yes, I do. / No, I don't.

2 your best friend / like / lizards
   _____
   _____

3 your friends / watch / TV
   _____
   _____

4 you / have / lunch at school
   _____
   _____

5 your school / have a big playground
   _____
   _____

5 Look at the pictures and answer the questions.

1 Does he like maths?
   No, he doesn't.

4 Does she get up at seven o'clock every morning?
   _____

2 Do they cook on Saturdays?
   _____

5 Do the children eat in the kitchen?
   _____

3 Do they wear hats in the classroom?
   _____

6 Does she go to the park?
   _____

6 Circle the correct words.

1 My cousin Sami **don't / doesn't** wear a helmet to school.
2 'Do you like sports?' 'Yes, I **do / don't**.'
3 It **don't / doesn't** snow in the summer.
4 'Do they go to the art club after school?' 'No, they **do / don't**.'
5 Mr Jones **don't / doesn't** teach history.
6 'Do children wear school uniforms in Argentina?' 'Yes, they **do / does**.'
7 'Does he like computer lessons?' 'No, he **don't / doesn't**.'
8 We **don't / doesn't** eat in the canteen every day.

7 Say it! Ask and answer questions with your partner about what you do and don't do every day. Use these suggestions to help you.

Do you have lunch at school every day?   *No, I don't.*

- walk to school?
- get up at seven o'clock?
- have lunch at school?
- play in a team?
- stay at home?
- meet your friends after school?

- every day
- every morning
- every afternoon
- every night
- at the weekend
- on Sundays, Mondays, etc.

Lesson 3

1 Read.

She never makes her bed.

She always makes her bed.

Adverbs of frequency

We use **adverbs of frequency** when we talk about habits or when we want to say how often something happens.

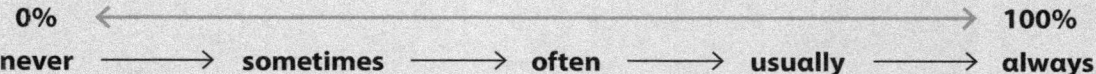

0% ← → 100%
never → sometimes → often → usually → always

Adverbs of frequency go before the main verb.
We **often** walk to school.
They **always** have lunch at one o'clock.

But they go after the verb **be**.
It is **usually** warm in the summer.
She is **often** at home on Wednesdays.

We use **How often ...?** to ask for more information about how frequently something happens.
How often do you write in your diary?
How often does Mum buy ice cream?

Time expressions
We can use the following time expressions to answer the question **How often ...?**
every day/week/weekend/month, once/twice/three times a day/week/month/year, etc.
How often do you cook?
Once a day.

33

2 Put the words in the correct order to make sentences or questions.

1 at / go / usually / we / to bed / nine o'clock
   We usually go to bed at nine o'clock.

2 never / Dad / works / weekend / at / the
   _____

3 ? / games / how often / you / play / do / video
   _____

4 usually / a test / have / on Tuesdays / we
   _____

5 ? / your mum / cook / how often / does
   _____

6 ? / they / how often / do / the park / to / go
   _____

3 Look at the table and complete the sentences.

	stays at home on Mondays	finishes school at three o'clock	wears jeans to school	reads comics in bed	talks to friends on the phone
Vicky	✓	✓✓✓✓	–	–	✓
Todd	✓✓	–	✓✓✓	✓	✓

1 Vicky ___never___ wears jeans to school.
2 Todd _____ reads comics in bed.
3 Todd _____ wears jeans to school.
4 Vicky and Todd _____ talk to friends on the phone.
5 Vicky _____ reads comics in bed.
6 Todd _____ finishes school at three o'clock.
7 Todd _____ stays at home on Mondays.
8 Vicky _____ finishes school at three o'clock.

never –
sometimes ✓
often ✓ ✓
usually ✓ ✓ ✓
always ✓ ✓ ✓ ✓

4 Choose the correct answers.

1 I don't like food in the morning. I _____ have breakfast.
   a never   **b** always

2 Paola loves books. She _____ goes to the library after school.
   a never   b usually

3 I'm scared of dogs. I _____ go near them.
   a always   b never

4 Lara likes games. She _____ buys them from the shop.
   a often   b never

5 Gaby plays the guitar. She _____ goes to the music club after school.
   a sometimes   b never

6 We only do sums in the lesson. Our teacher _____ gives us sums for homework.
   a often   b never

34 UNIT 3

5 Answer the questions so they are true for you. Use these adverbs of frequency.

always   never   often   sometimes   usually

1 How often do you walk to school?

2 How often do you see your grandparents?

3 How often do you study in the library?

4 How often do you watch films?

5 How often do you wear jeans to school?

6 How often do you talk to your friends on the phone?

7 How often do you sing in the music lesson?

8 How often do you have lunch at school?

6 Say it! Ask and answer questions with your partner. Use these suggestions to help you.

How often do you go to the beach?

I go to the beach twice a year.

- go to the beach?
- play a sport?
- see your best friend?
- cook?
- go on holiday?
- have an English lesson?
- eat burgers?
- go to the park?

- every day
- every week
- every weekend
- every month
- once/twice/three times a day
- once/twice/three times a week
- once/twice/three times a month
- once/twice/three times a year

35

Lesson 1

1 Read.

Where is Greece? Who can point to Greece?

Question words

We use **question words** when we want more information than just **yes** or **no** in the answer.
We use the following **question words**:

- **What** to ask about things or actions.
  What is this? It's a stamp collection.
  What do you do on Saturdays? I do my homework.
- **Who** to ask about people.
  Who is this? My friend Paul.
- **Where** to ask about position or place.
  Where is my guitar? It's on your bed.
- **Whose** to ask who something belongs to.
  Whose comic is it? It's my comic.
- **When** to ask about time.
  When is the art competition? It's on Friday.
- **Why** to ask about the reason for something.
  Why do you collect stamps? I think it's interesting.
- **Which** to ask about one person or thing within a group of similar people or things.
  Which pencil do you want? I want the blue one.
- **How** to ask about the way someone does something.
  How do you go to school? I go to school by bus.

When we use **question words** to ask about the subject of a sentence (the person, animal or thing that does the action), the word order does not change and the verb stays in the affirmative form.
Who lives here?
(**Sally** lives here.)
Whose drink is on the table?
(**Peter's** drink is on the table.)

When we use **question words** to ask about something other than the subject of a sentence, then the word order changes to the question form.
What do you eat in the morning?
(I eat **eggs**.)
Where do you stay in the summer?
(I stay at **my uncle's house**.)

Remember!

Be careful with these words:
Who's (who is) and **Whose** (asks who something belongs to).
Who's in the classroom?
Clare is in the classroom.
Whose skateboard is this?
It's Clare's skateboard.

2 Circle the correct words.

1 **What / Who** is your favourite singer?
2 **Whose / Who's** shop is this?
3 **When / What** do you go swimming?
4 **Which / How** bag do you like?
5 **Where / What** is the matter with Donna?
6 **Who / How** do you make a kite?
7 **Why / Which** do you do your homework at school?
8 **Who / Where** is the library?

3 Match.

1 When do you get up?
2 Where does he live?
3 Whose burger is this?
4 Who's the boy in school uniform?
5 What do students do after school?
6 How do you spell 'cat'?
7 Which ball do you want?
8 Why do you want a sandwich?

a It's George.
b The small one.
c C–A–T
d I'm hungry.
e Their homework.
f It's mine.
g At half past seven.
h In a beach house.

4 Look at the pictures and complete the questions with question words.

1 __When__ is Grandma's birthday? — It's in March.
2 _____ is this? — It's a coin.
3 _____ do you go on holiday? — I usually go to Spain.

4 _____ is that lady? — She's my teacher.
5 _____ present is this? — It's my sister's.
6 _____ do you play computer games? — I think they're exciting.

5 Put the words in the correct order to make questions.

1 the / is / Chinese lesson / when
   When is the Chinese lesson?

2 your / game / is / what / favourite
   _____

3 comics / these / whose / are
   _____

4 the puzzle / has got / who / a piece of
   _____

5 stay / in / where / you / do / the summer
   _____

6 cake / do / make / how / a / you
   _____

6 Look at the answers and complete the questions.

1 Who _____ comes from Brazil _____?
  Where _____ does Liz come from _____?
  Liz comes from Brazil.

2 Who _____?
  What _____?
  Tom likes puzzles.

3 What _____?
  When _____?
  The competition is on Friday.

4 Who _____?
  Where _____?
  Jamie and Helen live in Canada.

5 Whose _____?
  Where _____?
  Susan's laptop is in the classroom.

7 Say it! Ask and answer questions with your partner. Use these suggestions to help you.

- What is your favourite sport?
- What is your favourite hobby?
- When is your birthday?
- What do you usually have for breakfast?
- Where do you live?

Who is your best friend?

My best friend is Sally.

38 UNIT 4

Lesson 2

1 Read.

He can ride a bike, but he can't ride it very well.

Can

We use **can** to
- show ability.
  *We **can** sing.*
  ***Can** they speak French?*
- ask for or give permission to do something.
  ***Can** I go on the roller coaster?*
  *You **can** go to the park on Saturday.*

Can is followed by the bare infinitive.
We use **can** for the present and the future.
***Can** I go to the amusement park, Mum?*
*We **can** go swimming at the weekend.*

We often use **can** with verbs of feeling, such as **see**, **hear**, **smell**, etc.
*I **can** hear the roller coaster!*

We don't usually use **cannot** in everyday English.
But we sometimes use it to give emphasis.
*No, John, you **cannot** go to the park!*

Remember!

Bare infinitive = infinitive without **to**

Affirmative	Negative	Question	Short answers	
I can go.	I can't (cannot) go.	Can I go?	Yes, I can.	No, I can't.
You can go.	You can't (cannot) go.	Can you go?	Yes, you can.	No, you can't.
He can go.	He can't (cannot) go.	Can he go?	Yes, he can.	No, he can't.
She can go.	She can't (cannot) go.	Can she go?	Yes, she can.	No, she can't.
It can go.	It can't (cannot) go.	Can it go?	Yes, it can.	No, it can't.
We can go.	We can't (cannot) go.	Can we go?	Yes, we can.	No, we can't.
You can go.	You can't (cannot) go.	Can you go?	Yes, you can.	No, you can't.
They can go.	They can't (cannot) go.	Can they go?	Yes, they can.	No, they can't.

2 Complete the sentences with *can* or *can't*.

1 Teddy bears __can't__ speak.
2 Penguins _____ swim.
3 Babies _____ ride bicycles.
4 Sharks __can't__ fly.
5 Spiders _____ move fast.
6 Computers _____ cook.

3 Complete the sentences using *can* or *can't* and the words in brackets.

1 __Can__ he __cook__ Chinese food? (cook)
2 Students _____ comics in the classroom. (read)
3 _____ we _____ to the amusement park? (go)
4 Bobby _____ a computer, because he hasn't got any money. (buy)
5 It's very cold. You _____ today. (swim)
6 We _____ lunch in the canteen. (have)

4 Look at the pictures and write sentences about them. Use *can* or *can't*.

1 they / cook
   They can cook.

4 you / eat here

2 the dog / come in

5 the baby / do the puzzle

3 Dina / play the guitar

6 the girls / see the park from the Ferris wheel

5 **Write questions using *can*. Answer them.**

1 penguins / fly
   <u>Can penguins fly?</u>
   <u>No, they can't.</u>

2 your brother / play the piano
   _____
   _____

3 robots / talk
   _____
   _____

4 your dad / make a cake
   _____
   _____

5 your mum / speak Spanish
   _____
   _____

6 chimpanzees / read books
   _____
   _____

6 **Look at the picture and answer the questions.**

1 Can Mum read her book?
   <u>Yes, she can.</u>

2 Can the boy fly a kite?
   _____

3 Can the baby play with his toys?
   _____

4 Can the girl ride her bike?
   _____

5 Can Dad catch any fish?
   _____

6 Can the girls see any birds?
   _____

7 **Say it! Ask and answer questions with a partner about what you can or can't do. Use these suggestions to help you.**

Can you speak English?   Yes, I can.

- make a kite
- ride a bike
- have chocolate for breakfast
- use a laptop
- play the guitar
- speak Chinese
- make a cake
- stay up late at the weekend

Review

1 Circle the correct words.

1 The library doesn't **opens / (open)** at nine o'clock.
2 Dad **carries / carry** my baby brother to the park.
3 The children **do / does** their homework in the kitchen.
4 We **don't / doesn't** dance in the music lesson.
5 The students at my school **reads / read** lots of books.
6 I **enjoys / enjoy** art lessons.
7 Mum doesn't **works / work** at the weekend.
8 Our teacher **tidy / tidies** the classroom every afternoon.

2 Complete the questions using the words in brackets. Then complete the short answers.

1 _Does it snow_ in summer? (it / snow)   No, _it doesn't_.
2 _____ a helmet to work? (Dad / wear)   Yes, _____.
3 _____ comics at the canteen? (they / sell)   No, _____.
4 _____ your kite on the beach? (you / fly)   Yes, _____.
5 _____ ice skating on Saturdays? (she / go)   No, _____.
6 _____ our geography books? (we / need)   Yes, _____.

3 Look at the answers and complete the questions.

1 Who _lives in Canada_?
   Where _does Cathy live_?
   Cathy lives in Canada.

2 What _____?
   When _____?
   The party is on Saturday.

3 Whose _____?
   Where _____?
   Mr Smith's car is in the garage.

4 Who _____?
   What _____?
   Tom wants to buy a skateboard.

5 Who _____?
   Why _____?
   Paul is sad because he has got a test.

6 Who _____?
   When _____?
   Marla calls her grandma on Saturdays.

4 Put the words in the correct order to make sentences.

1 her cousins / visits / Daniella / sometimes / on Saturdays
 On Saturdays, Daniella sometimes visits her cousins.

2 goes shopping / Susan / on Fridays / with her friends / often
_____

3 every night / takes his dog / usually / for a walk / Paul
_____

4 at the weekend / sometimes / I / ride my horse
_____

5 never / Jill / in winter / goes swimming
_____

6 play / Judy and Simone / with their doll's house / usually / after school
_____

5 Look at the pictures and complete the sentences with *can* or *can't*.

1 Tommy ____can____ play tennis.

2 Fish _____ walk.

3 My friends _____ dance.

4 Mum _____ use a laptop.

5 They _____ find the sports centre.

6 Liz _____ play the piano.

6 Complete the dialogue with these words.

~~how~~   what   when   where   which   who   whose   why

Tina: Hi, Lilly. (1) ___How___ are you?
Lilly: I'm fine, thank you. Can I ring you later? I'm not at home now.
Tina: Oh, (2) _____ are you?
Lilly: I'm in a shop. I need to buy a birthday present.
Tina: (3) _____ birthday is it?
Lilly: It's Michelle's birthday tomorrow.
Tina: (4) _____ Michelle?
Lilly: My cousin Michelle.
Tina: Oh, yes! (5) _____ do you want to buy her?
Lilly: I don't know. Have you got any ideas?
Tina: (6) _____ do the shops close?
Lilly: Um, six o'clock I think. (7) _____ do you want to know?
Tina: Because I can come and meet you. We can buy her present together.
Lilly: Great idea! We are outside the music shop.
Tina: We? (8) _____ are you with?
Lilly: I'm with Rosie.
Tina: OK. See you soon!

WRITING PROJECT

7 Look at a project about a famous building. Complete the project with these words.

can   can't   hear   ~~think~~   usually   visit

The Taj Mahal

Most people (1) ___think___ of the Taj Mahal when they (2) _____ the word India. It's not surprising; it is the most famous building in India.

The Taj Mahal is a beautiful white marble building. There is a big garden around it, and there is a water tank in the centre of the garden.

The Taj Mahal is one of the seven wonders of the new world. Many people (3) _____ it every year. They (4) _____ visit in October, November and February because it isn't very hot then. Visitors (5) _____ take many things into the Taj Mahal. They (6) _____ only take water, a small camera and a mobile phone.

8 Now it's your turn to do a project about a famous building in your country. Find or draw a picture of the building and write about it.

Lesson 1 — 5

1 Read.

Imperative

We use the **imperative** when
- we give instructions or orders.
  Cut the cake, Paul!
- we want to prevent something.
  Don't move! There's a spider over there.

We form the imperative with the bare infinitive. We don't use a subject pronoun. The imperative is the same whether we are talking to one person or to many people.
Do your homework, Mary.
Mum, Dad, **buy** me some candles!
Get up! It's late.

We form the negative with the word **don't**.
Don't draw on the desk!

Remember!

We often use the word **please** so that we are more polite.
Open the door, **please**.
Please buy a birthday card for Sally.

2 Complete the sentences with the imperative. Use the verbs in brackets.

1 __Don't swim__ in that water! (not swim)
2 _____ careful on the rides! (be)
3 _____ to bed. It's midnight! (go)
4 _____ that! It's paint! (not touch)
5 _____ lunch for me. I've got a sandwich. (not make)
6 _____ your teeth, please. (brush)
7 _____ there. That's my seat. (not sit)
8 _____ your books away. (put)

3 Look at the pictures and complete the sentences with the correct imperative form of these verbs.

drink   finish   go   play   ~~throw~~   write

1 <u>Don't throw</u> the ball in the lake!
2 _____ to bed at eight o'clock.
3 _____ in the library, please.
4 _____ your homework now.
5 _____ your name here.
6 _____ your guitar at night!

Object pronouns

We use **object pronouns** to replace the object of a sentence. Objects are words (nouns, pronouns) that usually come after the verb.
*Look at the balloons! Look at **them**!*
*Can I open the present? Can I open **it**?*

Subject pronouns	Object pronouns
I	me
you	you
he	him
she	her
it	it
we	us
you	you
they	them

4 Complete the sentences with object pronouns.

1 Dance with ___me___ , please! (I)
2 Mum made a costume for _____ . (he)
3 Throw the ball to _____ . (we)
4 Open the door for _____ , please. (they)
5 Give the phone to _____ . (she)
6 Can I come shopping with _____ ? (you)

5 Complete the sentences with object pronouns.

1 Where's my uniform? I can't find ___it___ .
2 Those are my stamps. Give _____ to me!
3 I need a calculator. Find one for _____ , please.
4 We're hungry. Buy two burgers for _____ .
5 She's a good dancer. Look at _____ .
6 They're tourists. Ask _____ where they're from.

Let's

We use **Let's** with the bare infinitive to suggest something.
Let's have lunch at Sarah's house.
Let's make a birthday cake for Vicky.

We form the negative with the word **not**.
Let's not go to the park today.
Let's not go swimming in the sea.

Remember!

Bare infinitive = infinitive without **to**.

---

6 Complete the sentences using *Let's* or *Let's not* and the words in brackets.

1 ___Let's go___ to the film festival. I love films. (go)
2 _____ our bikes. It's boring. (ride)
3 _____ a party. It's your birthday! (have)
4 _____ lunch in the garden. It's cold. (have)
5 _____ our faces for the party! It's fun! (paint)
6 _____ to this music. I don't like it. (listen)

7 Match.

1 What can we do this weekend?
2 The tourists can't speak Greek.
3 Those are Paul's balloons.
4 There are sharks in this sea.
5 We need to decorate the house for the party.
6 We need some candles for the cake.

a Let's not swim here.
b Let's not go to the cinema again.
c Speak to them in English.
d Don't give them to John.
e Let's get them from Dad's shop.
f Let's get some balloons.

8 Say it! Make arrangements for the weekend with your partner. Use these suggestions to help you.

Let's go to the park on Saturday morning.

OK, and in the afternoon, let's go to the shops.

- watch a DVD
- go to the amusement park
- go for a walk
- have a party
- play basketball
- go bowling

Lesson 2

1 Read.

He's got two loaves of bread.

Countable and uncountable nouns

Countable nouns are nouns that we can count. They have both singular and plural forms. When the subject of a sentence is in the plural, then the verb must also be in the plural.
*Sam's ball **is** blue.*
*The balls **are** green.*

Uncountable nouns are nouns that we cannot count. They don't have plural forms. When the subject of a sentence is an uncountable noun, then the verb must be in the singular.
*John's got lots of **work**.*
*Ice cream **is** delicious.*

We can use expressions such as: **a piece of**, **a slice of**, **a cup of**, **a glass of**, **a carton of**, **a loaf of**, etc. to show how much we have of something.
*I've got **a piece of** cake.*
***Two cups of** coffee, please.*

Remember!

We don't use **a** or **an** with uncountable nouns.

2 Complete the table with these nouns.

~~animal~~   clown   ~~fun~~   hair   laptop   map
money   music   party   robot   time   work

Countable		Uncountable	
animal	_____	fun	_____
_____	_____	_____	_____
_____	_____	_____	_____

48 UNIT 5

3 **Look at the pictures and complete the sentences.**

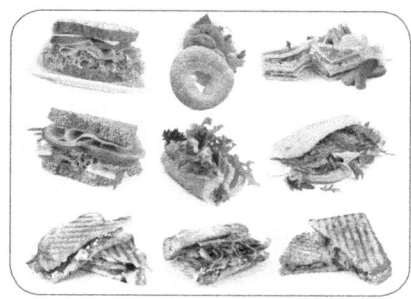

1 I'm hungry. Let's make some ___sandwiches___.

4 Sandra has got long _____.

2 We need red _____ for the party.

5 Wow! That's a lot of _____!

3 My sister's favourite food is _____.

6 Mum, we must buy some _____ for the twins.

4 **Choose the correct answers.**

1 Our teacher always gives us _____ homework.
   a a   (b) -

2 Wow! Look at the _____ at this party!
   a food   b foods

3 This is _____ great film!
   a -   b a

4 Oh no! I've got paint in my _____!
   a hair   b hairs

5 _____ there music at the carnival?
   a Are   b Is

6 Have you got _____ costume for the carnival?
   a -   b a

5 Look at the pictures and complete the phrases with one of these expressions.

> a carton of   a cup of   a glass of   a loaf of   ~~a packet of~~   a slice of

1 ___a packet of___ crisps

4 _____ lemonade

2 _____ milk

5 _____ bread

3 _____ pizza

6 _____ coffee

6 Say it! Talk to your partner about what things you've got. Use these suggestions to help you.
- in your school bag
- in your bedroom
- in your fridge

I've got lots of books in my bag.

I've got an apple and an orange.

50 UNIT 5

Lesson 3

1 Read.

There are some vegetables and there is some fruit. There isn't any cake.

Some, any

We use **some** in affirmative sentences with uncountable nouns and plural countable nouns to say that something exists.
There are **some** toys in the box.
There's **some** food in the kitchen.

We use **any** in negative sentences and questions with uncountable nouns and plural countable nouns to say that something doesn't exist or to ask if something exists.
Are there **any** drinks on the table?
I haven't got **any** homework today.

Remember!

We can use the word **some** in questions when we ask for or offer something.
Can I have **some** money, please?
Can I get you **some** coffee?

2 Choose the correct answers.

1 There aren't _____ DVDs in the room.
   a some   (b) any

2 We've got _____ lemonade in our bags.
   a any   b some

3 _____ any tickets for the play.
   a There are   b There aren't

4 Do you watch _____ TV after dinner?
   a any   b some

5 Has the clown got _____ balloons?
   a some   b any

6 _____ any kites in the shop?
   a Is there   b Are there

7 Please send us _____ invitations.
   a any   b some

8 _____ any sharks in the sea.
   a There are   b There aren't

3 Complete the sentences with *some* or *any*.

1 I need ___some___ candles for the cake.
2 Have you got _____ friends in Australia?
3 There aren't _____ good costumes this year.
4 Are you hungry? We've got _____ burgers.
5 Are there _____ monsters in the film?
6 He hasn't got _____ solutions to the problem.
7 He needs _____ money to buy presents.
8 There aren't _____ masks in the shop.
9 We need _____ food for the festival.

4 Look at the pictures and complete the sentences using *some* or *any* and the words given.

1 snow / the beach
   There isn't ___any snow on the beach___ .

4 rides / amusement park
   There are _____ .

2 maps / classroom
   There aren't _____ .

5 food / the plate
   There is _____ .

3 presents / the table
   Are there _____ ?

6 fruit / bowl
   There is _____ .

52 UNIT 5

5 **Complete the dialogue with *some* or *any*.**

Veronica: It's carnival time! Have you got a costume?

Graciana: Yes, I have. I've got two costumes. One for me and one for you, but I haven't got (1) ___any___ hats.

Veronica: I've got (2) _____ hats. They're my brother's. We always like the hats and masks!

Graciana: Wait, I've got an idea!

Veronica: I have, too. Let's buy (3) _____ balloons.

Graciana: No, we don't need (4) _____ balloons. Dad buys them for us every year. Let's get (5) _____ paint, paper and glue.

Veronica: We don't need (6) _____ paint, paper or glue for the carnival, Graciana!

Graciana: Oh, yes we do. Let's make our own masks!

Veronica: Great idea!

6 **Say it! Ask and answer questions with your partner about what there is at your school. Use these suggestions to help you.**

- paint
- coffee
- art lessons
- lemonade
- computers
- ice cream
- balloons
- food
- comics
- canteen

Are there any computers at your school?

Yes, there are.

6 Lesson 1

1 Read.

Much, many

We use **much** and **many** to describe quantity. We use **much** with uncountable nouns mainly in negative sentences and questions.
*There isn't **much** cheese in my sandwich.*
*Have you got **much** time?*

We use **many** with plural countable nouns mainly in negative sentences and questions.
*There aren't **many** waiters in the restaurant.*
*Are there **many** glasses on the table?*

We use **How much ...?** and **How many ...?** when we ask about quantity. We use **How much ...?** for uncountable nouns and **How many ...?** for countable nouns.
How much fruit do you eat?
How many plates are there?

Remember!

We usually don't use **much** and **many** in affirmative sentences. We use **a lot of** or **lots of** instead.
*She's got **a lot of** / **lots of** friends.*
*Dean drinks **a lot of** / **lots of** water.*

2 Circle the correct words.

1 Are there **much** / **(many)** oranges on the tree?
2 He hasn't got **much** / **many** work to do today.
3 The amusement park is boring. There aren't **much** / **many** rides.
4 She doesn't have **much** / **many** snacks.
5 There aren't **much** / **many** desserts on the menu.
6 The man in the café hasn't got **much** / **many** hair.
7 Are there **much** / **many** children in the parade?
8 There isn't **much** / **many** pizza on the plate.

3 Look at the pictures and complete the sentences with *much* or *many*.

1 There isn't __much__ ketchup.

2 There aren't _____ people at the café.

3 There isn't _____ water in the glass.

4 There aren't _____ drinks on this menu.

5 There aren't _____ pieces in this puzzle.

6 There isn't _____ ice in this drink.

4 Complete the questions with *How much* or *How many*.

1 ____How many____ candles are there on the cake?
2 _____ food do we need for the party?
3 _____ glasses are there on the kitchen table?
4 _____ fast food restaurants are there in your town?
5 _____ cheese do we need for the sandwiches?
6 _____ milk do you drink in the morning?
7 _____ people go to the food festival every year?
8 _____ money do we need for the carnival costumes?

5 Say it! Ask and answer questions with your partner about what you eat and drink. Use these suggestions to help you.

- milk / for breakfast?
- fruit / in the evening?
- meat / for dinner?
- sandwich / at school?
- water / every day?
- biscuit / every day?

How many meals do you have a day?

I usually have three.

Lesson 2

1 Read.

There are lots of sweets on the table, but there's only a little fruit.

A lot of, lots of, a few, a little

We use **a lot of** or **lots of** with countable and uncountable nouns in affirmative and negative sentences and in questions.
*We've got **lots of** food.*
*He hasn't got **a lot of** toys.*
*Have you got **lots of** friends?*

We use **a few** with plural countable nouns in affirmative sentences and in questions to show that a small number of something exists. It has a positive meaning.
*She's got **a few** friends in China.*
*Do you want **a few** chips?*

We use **a little** with uncountable nouns in affirmative sentences and in questions to show that a small amount of something exists. It has a positive meaning.
*There is **a little** mustard.*
*Can I have **a little** juice, please?*

2 Choose the correct answers.

1 They've got _____ DVDs.
  a a little   (b) a lot of

2 I've got _____ good friends.
  a a few   b a little

3 There are _____ magazines on the table.
  a a little   b a few

4 For breakfast, I usually drink _____ apple juice.
  a a little   b a few

5 There's _____ food on the table.
  a a lot of   b a few

6 Suzie eats _____ meat every day.
  a a few   b a little

7 There are _____ Indian restaurants in the city.
  a lots of   b a little

8 My brother eats _____ chicken.
  a a few   b lots of

3 Look at the pictures and complete the sentences with *a few*, *a little*, *a lot of* or *lots of*.

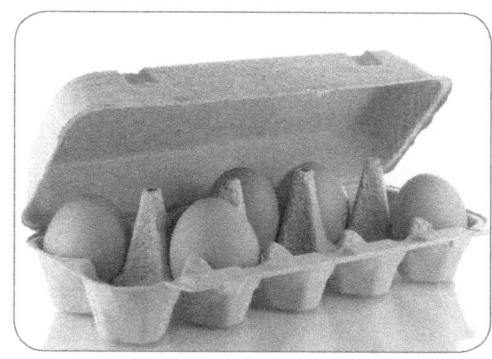

1 Nancy has got a lot of / lots of apples.

4 There are _____ eggs in the box.

2 I've got _____ chocolate.

5 There's _____ juice in the glass.

3 There are _____ holes in the cheese.

6 There are _____ chips on the plate.

4 Complete the sentences with *a few* or *a little*.

1 There's a little milk in the glass.
2 Can I have _____ ketchup, please?
3 Let's have _____ biscuits with our orange juice.
4 Can we have _____ chips with our sandwich?
5 There are _____ knives on the table.
6 Is there _____ rice for me?
7 Marco always has _____ cheese on his bread.
8 Let's buy _____ carrots for our carrot cake.

57

5 **Put the words in the correct order to make sentences or questions.**

1 a few / we've / tomatoes / got
   We've got a few tomatoes.

2 coffee / want / a little / I / in / milk / my
   _____

3 ? / fish / lots of / they / do / in Spain / eat
   _____

4 for / need / a little / we / cake / the / butter
   _____

5 ? / people / are / the restaurant / in / there / a lot of
   _____

6 a little / drinks / he / with / lunch / his / juice
   _____

7 ? / children / in / a lot of / are / the / there / classroom
   _____

8 lots of / under / are / table / there / the / presents
   _____

6 **Say it! Talk to your partner about what you and your family buy at the supermarket. Use these suggestions to help you.**

We buy lots of fruit.

We buy a few cakes.

- a few
- a little
- a lot of
- lots of

- apples
- bananas
- cakes
- cheese
- chicken
- chocolate

- fish
- juice
- meat
- milk
- rice
- water

Review

1 Complete the sentences with the imperative. Use the verbs in brackets.

1 ____Finish____ your homework, please! (finish)
2 _____ this snack before lunch. (not eat)
3 _____ home late tonight. (not come)
4 _____ to buy the eggs! (not forget)
5 _____ me some pasta for dinner, please. (make)
6 _____ a bottle of orange juice for the party, please. (buy)

2 Complete the sentences using *Let's* or *Let's not* and the verbs in brackets.

1 It's carnival time! ____Let's wear____ our masks. (wear)
2 It's very cold outside. _____ skateboarding in the park. (go)
3 We've got a geography test tomorrow. _____ to the library to study. (go)
4 The cat is hungry. _____ it some food. (give)
5 Marco eats Italian food every day! _____ spaghetti for him. (make)
6 She's sad. _____ her a joke. (tell)

3 Complete the sentences with *some* or *any*.

1 Is there ____any____ sugar in your tea?
2 She's got _____ fruit in her bag.
3 Don't buy _____ ice cream.
4 Look! I can see _____ people in the sea!
5 I've got _____ snacks for our picnic.
6 There aren't _____ twins in my class this year.

4 Complete the sentences with object pronouns.

1 Give the knife to ____me____, please. (I)
2 I sit next to _____ at school. (she)
3 Dad loves fireworks. We always go to see them with _____. (he)
4 We've got the invitations with _____. (we)
5 Is Madeleine at the music festival with _____? (you)
6 I often send text messages to _____. (Aunt Sue and Uncle Dean)
7 I can't find my costume for the carnival. Where is _____? (it)

5 Complete the questions with *How much* or *How many*.

1 __How many__ cartons of milk are there?
2 _____ cheese do we need for the spaghetti?
3 _____ tea does he drink every day?
4 _____ stalls are there at the festival?
5 _____ rides can you see?
6 _____ homework have we got today?

6 Circle the correct answers.

1 I want to send John **-** / **an** invitation.
2 There's **a** / **-** treasure hunt in the park today.
3 My cousin Lucy has got **a** / **-** lovely hair.
4 He's got **an** / **-** unusual coin in his collection.
5 Sam sends me **an** / **-** email every day.
6 We often eat **a** / **-** Chinese food.
7 I usually have **a** / **-** cheese sandwich for lunch.
8 Most people really like **a** / **-** chocolate.

7 Look at the pictures and choose the correct answers.

1 There are _____ bananas at the stall.
   a lots of
   b a few

2 There's _____ jam in the jar.
   a a little
   b a lot of

3 There are _____ clowns at the parade.
   a a little
   b a lot of

4 We've got _____ masks for the fancy-dress party.
   a a little
   b lots of

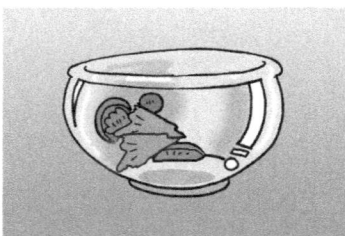

5 There's only _____ salad in the bowl.
   a a lot of
   b a little

6 There are _____ people at the carnival.
   a lots of
   b a little

8 Complete the dialogue with these phrases.

> a carton of   ~~a cup of~~   a glass of   a jar of   a loaf of   a packet of   a slice of

Mum: May, help me serve our visitors, please.

May: OK, Mum. What do you need?

Mum: Um, (1) __a cup of__ coffee for Mr Lewis, and (2) _____ apple juice for his wife, please.

May: OK. Does Mr Lewis take milk and sugar?

Mum: Milk, yes, but no sugar. There's (3) _____ milk in the fridge.

May: Mum, let's give them (4) _____ cake, too.

Mum: Yes, you're right. There's also (5) _____ biscuits in the cupboard. Put some on a plate, please.

May: OK. Mum, I'm hungry. Have we got any sandwiches?

Mum: Well, there's (6) _____ bread on the table.

May: Great, and there's (7) _____ honey in the cupboard.

Mum: Honey sandwiches, May?

May: Yes, they're delicious!

WRITING PROJECT

9 Look at a project about the Great Barrier Reef. Complete the project with these words.

> don't   few   let's   lots   ~~many~~   remember   some   some

The Great Barrier Reef

The Great Barrier Reef is near the coast of Queensland, Australia. It is home to (1) __many__ kinds of sea creatures. People from all over the world visit the reef every year.

There are more than 400 kinds of coral and about 1,500 kinds of fish. (2) _____ fish can change their colours to hide from an enemy. There are also (3) _____ of different whales and dolphins. Sometimes visitors see a (4) _____ playing in the sea. These clownfish usually live in pairs. These are just (5) _____ of the animals that live on the reef.

The Great Barrier Reef is a very special place. (6) _____ protect it. (7) _____ , when you visit, (8) _____ throw rubbish into the sea!

clownfish

10 Now it's your turn to do a project about a famous place in your country. Find or draw a picture of the place and write about it.

Lesson 1

1 Read.

They're running a race.

Present continuous affirmative

We use the **present continuous** for actions that
- are in progress at the time of speaking.
  *Robbie and Jake **are running** in the race.*
- are in progress around the time of speaking.
  These days, everyone is using the Internet.
- are temporary.
  ***She's living** in London at the moment.*

We form the affirmative with **am**, **are** or **is** and the main verb with the **–ing** ending.
*read   read**ing***

When the main verb ends in **–e**, we take off the **–e** and add **–ing**.
*chase   chas**ing***

When the verb ends in a vowel + consonant, we double the final consonant and add **–ing**.
*win   win**ning***

When the verb ends in **–ie**, we take off the **–ie** and add **–y** and **–ing**.
*lie   l**ying***

When the verb ends in **–l**, we double the **–l** and add **–ing**.
*travel travel**ling***

Time expressions
We often use the following time expressions with the **present continuous**: now, at the moment, these days, this year, today, tonight, etc.
*I **am writing** a letter **at the moment**.*
*Monica **is working** a lot **these days**.*
*Simon **is staying** with his grandparents **tonight**.*

Affirmative
I'm falling (I am falling)
you're falling (you are falling)
he's falling (he is falling)
she's falling (she is falling)
it's falling (it is falling)
we're falling (we are falling)
you're falling (you are falling)
they're falling (they are falling)

2 **Complete the table.**

fall → falling	write → writing	cut → cutting
play →	have →	win →
climb →	dance →	get →
enter →	leave →	put →
push →	make →	sit →
sail →	practise →	stop →

3 **Complete the sentences with the present continuous. Use the verbs in brackets.**

1 We _____'re/are working_____ on the computer. (work)

2 Look! Terry _____ a kite. (fly)

3 Tom _____ his bike. (fix)

4 Sally _____ the laptop. (use)

5 I _____ for my test. (study)

6 Mum and Dad _____ around Australia. (travel)

4 **Complete the sentences with the present continuous. Use these verbs.**

do   move   run   ~~walk~~   wear   write

1 I _____'m/am walking_____ to school today.

2 Dimitra _____ a helmet.

3 The robot _____ its hands!

4 I _____ an email to Uncle Bob.

5 Maria _____ in the race.

6 Carlo and Mario _____ the puzzle.

5 **Put the words in the correct order to make sentences.**

1 are / fast / they / running / very
   They are running very fast.

2 race / Todd / entering / the / is
   _____

3 park / are / we / the / sitting / in
   _____

4 her / she / doing / is / homework
   _____

5 Mandy / are / and / volleyball / Dad / playing
   _____

63

6 Look at the pictures and complete the sentences with the present continuous. Use these verbs.

climb   ~~cross~~   dive   give   ride   sail

1 Chao ___is crossing___ the finish line.

4 They _____ to an island.

2 He _____ .

5 The teacher _____ him a prize.

3 They _____ a mountain.

6 Sara _____ a horse.

7 Say it! Point to the children. Ask and answer questions with your partner about what they are doing.

What is this girl doing?

She's reading a book.

64   UNIT 7

Lesson 2

1 Read.

I can't find the cat. Is it sleeping?

No, Mum. The cat isn't sleeping. It's eating the fish!

Oh, no! That's today's dinner!

Present continuous negative and questions

In the negative form, we use **am**, **are** or **is**, the word **not** and the main verb with the **–ing** ending.
*I **am not** work**ing**.*
*You **are not** listen**ing**.*
*Mel **is not** play**ing**.*

In the question form, we use **am**, **are** or **is**, and the main verb with the **–ing** ending.
***Am** I wear**ing** your hat?*
***Are** you listen**ing** to the radio?*
***Is** Julie cook**ing** dinner?*

In short answers, we only use **am**, **are** or **is**. We don't use the main verb.
***Am** I do**ing** my homework?*
*Yes, you **are**.*
***Are** you enjoy**ing** the party?*
*No, **I'm not**.*
***Are** Amanda and Paul watch**ing** TV?*
*Yes, they **are**.*

Negative	Question	Short answers	
I'm not falling (I am not falling)	Am I falling?	Yes, I am.	No, I'm not.
you aren't falling (you are not falling)	Are you falling?	Yes, you are.	No, you aren't.
he isn't falling (he is not falling)	Is he falling?	Yes, he is.	No, he isn't.
she isn't falling (she is not falling)	Is she falling?	Yes, she is.	No, she isn't.
it isn't falling (it is not falling)	Is it falling?	Yes, it is.	No, it isn't.
we aren't falling (we are not falling)	Are we falling?	Yes, we are.	No, we aren't.
you aren't falling (you are not falling)	Are you falling?	Yes, you are.	No, you aren't.
they aren't falling (they are not falling)	Are they falling?	Yes, they are.	No, they aren't.

2 Write negative sentences.

1 Juan / ride a horse
   Juan isn't riding a horse.

2 Daiyu / dive
   _____

3 Aisha / wear boots
   _____

4 We / ride our bicycles
   _____

5 Jon and Anna / get ready
   _____

6 The gymnast / train
   _____

3 Look at the pictures and answer the questions.

1 Is she drinking orange juice?
   No, she isn't.

2 Is the dog chasing a cat?
   _____

3 Are they training for a race?
   _____

4 Are they diving?
   _____

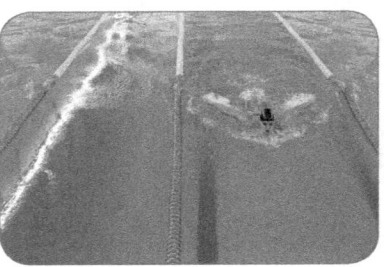

5 Is the swimmer training for the competition?
   _____

6 Is she climbing a mountain?
   _____

4 Complete the questions with the present continuous using the words in brackets. Then complete the short answers.

1. ___Is she riding___ her bike? (she / ride)
   Yes, ___she is___ .
2. _____ a tennis match? (he / watch)
   No, _____ .
3. _____ scared now? (you / feel)
   No, _____ .
4. _____ in the team? (they / play)
   Yes, _____ .
5. _____ the ball? (the football player / kick)
   Yes, _____ .
6. _____ to the sports centre? (we / walk)
   No, _____ .

5 Complete the dialogue with the present continuous. Use these verbs.

> call   ~~do~~   get ready   not do   train   watch

Speaker 1: Hi. (1) ___Are___ you ___doing___ your homework?
Speaker 2: No, I (2) _____ homework! I (3) _____ TV. What about you?
Speaker 1: I (4) _____ to go swimming with my brother. We've got a swimming competition next week.
Speaker 2: (5) _____ you _____?
Speaker 1: Yes, we are – every day! We've got to be ready. Oh, I've got to go. My brother (6) _____ me.

6 Say it! Take turns with your partner to mime a sport or activity. Your partner must guess what you are doing. Use these suggestions to help you.

> Are you skateboarding?

> No, I'm not.

- boxing
- cycling
- diving
- playing football
- playing tennis
- playing volleyball
- running
- swimming
- climbing

Lesson 3

1 Read.

They're going on holiday tomorrow.

Present continuous (to express the future)

We use the **present continuous** to talk about our plans for the near future.

We always use time expressions with the **present continuous** when we are talking about the future.
I **am playing** in a football match **on Saturday**.
We **are meeting** at the sports centre **tonight**.

When asking and answering questions about future plans, time expressions are sometimes just used in the question.
What **are you doing tomorrow**?
I**'m skating** with my sister.

2 Complete the sentences with the present continuous. Use the verbs in brackets.

1 I ___'m/am washing___ my dad's car this evening. (wash)

2 Chen _____ a guitar lesson today. (have)

3 _____ you _____ dinner tonight? (make)

4 Dai and I _____ our grandma at the weekend. (not visit)

5 Amir and Reza _____ in the race tomorrow. (not take part)

6 _____ Mel _____ on holiday this summer? (go)

7 We _____ to Lisbon this afternoon. (fly)

8 I _____ tonight. (not study)

3 Complete the letter with the present continuous. Use the verbs in brackets.

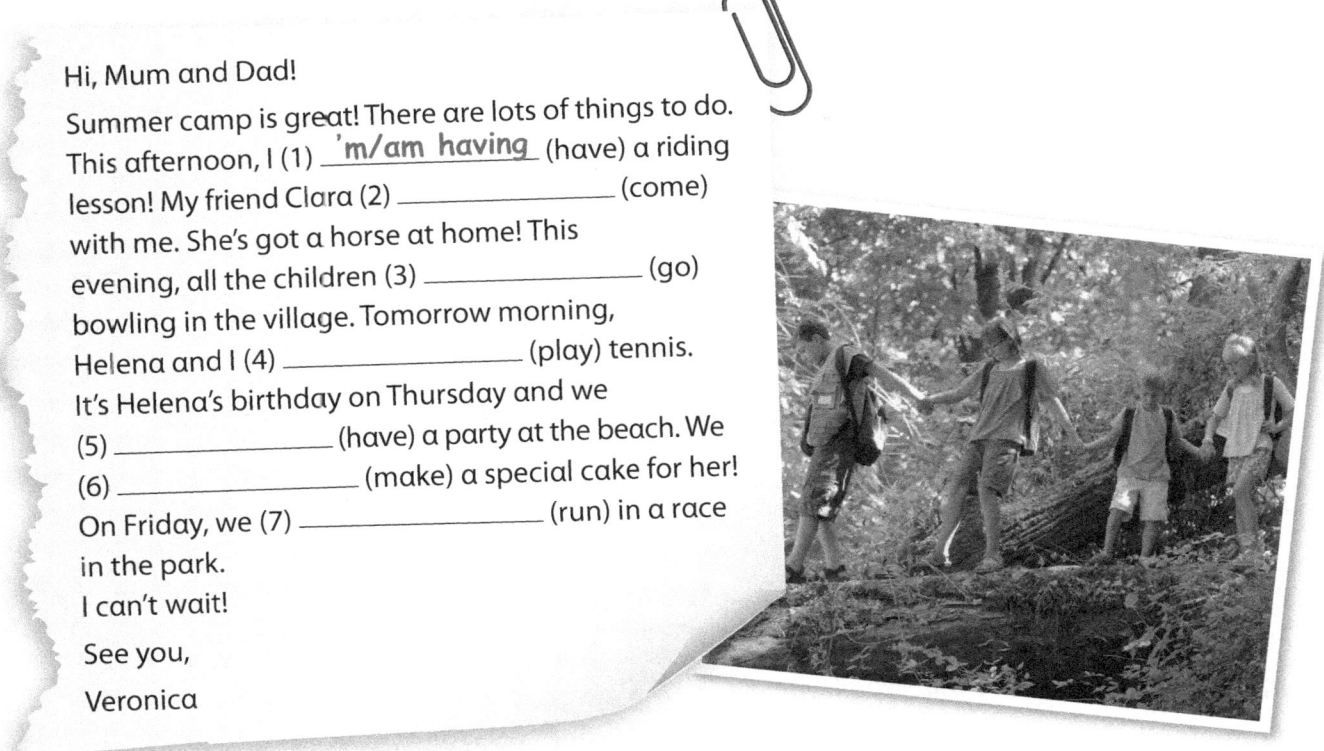

Hi, Mum and Dad!

Summer camp is great! There are lots of things to do. This afternoon, I (1) _'m/am having_ (have) a riding lesson! My friend Clara (2) _____ (come) with me. She's got a horse at home! This evening, all the children (3) _____ (go) bowling in the village. Tomorrow morning, Helena and I (4) _____ (play) tennis. It's Helena's birthday on Thursday and we (5) _____ (have) a party at the beach. We (6) _____ (make) a special cake for her! On Friday, we (7) _____ (run) in a race in the park.
I can't wait!
See you,
Veronica

4 Look at the pictures and complete the sentences about Daniela's and Eduardo's plans. Use the present continuous.

1 On Friday morning, Daniela _is buying a present_ .
2 On Friday afternoon, Daniela _____ .
3 On Friday afternoon, Eduardo _____ .
4 On Saturday morning, Daniela _____ .
5 On Saturday morning, Eduardo _____ .
6 On Saturday evening, Daniela and Eduardo _____ .

5 Complete the dialogue with the present continuous. Use these verbs.

> buy   come   go   go   have   meet   train   watch

Ahmed: Let's go to the sports centre one day this week. There are basketball matches every day.
Malik: OK. Mmm, let me think.
Ahmed: Can you go this afternoon?
Malik: No, I (1) ____'m/am going____ mountain climbing with Dad.
Ahmed: Wow! That's exciting. Let's go tomorrow afternoon. There's a match at four o'clock.
Malik: I can't. Tomorrow afternoon, I (2) _____ for the tennis competition next week. Can we go in the evening?
Ahmed: Oh dear. I can't. I (3) _____ the Olympic Games on TV with my family. My cousin (4) _____ at five o'clock.
Malik: Well, on Wednesday afternoon, I (5) _____ tickets for the skating championship, but I can go in the evening.
Ahmed: Oh, on Wednesday evening, I (6) _____ my friend Clara. She's got my brother's mask and he needs it. He (7) _____ diving at the weekend.
Malik: Let's go on Thursday.
Ahmed: On Thursday, we (8) _____ a party after school.
Malik: Yes, at three o'clock. We can go to the sports centre in the evening.
Ahmed: You're right. Great!

6 Say it! Ask and answer questions with your partner about your plans for the weekend. Use these suggestions to help you.

> What are you doing on Saturday morning?

> I'm going shopping with Mum.

- do homework
- go for a walk
- go shopping
- listen to music
- meet friends

- play video games
- play a sport
- read a book
- ride my bike
- watch TV

Lesson 1 8

1 Read.

Emma's mum usually makes breakfast for her, but today she is making breakfast for her mum.

Present simple and present continuous

We use the **present simple** to talk about
- general truths.
  It **is** very hot in the desert.
- things that we do regularly.
  We **go** to the park every Saturday.
- permanent situations.
  My grandparents **live** in Australia.

We use the **present continuous** for actions that
- are in progress at the time of speaking.
  Cathy and John **are playing** a game.
- are in progress around the time of speaking.
  She**'s living** in London at the moment.
- are temporary.
  My friend **is working** in a shop.

Remember!

We use different **time expressions** with the **present simple** (see page 27) and with the **present continuous** (see page 62).

2 Complete the table.

Present simple	Present continuous
always	at present

~~always~~	on Fridays
~~at present~~	sometimes
at the moment	this week
every day	this year
never	today
now	usually

71

3 Write sentences with the present simple and the present continuous.

1 on Saturdays / we / usually / have / lunch at home
   but today / we / have / lunch in a restaurant
   <u>On Saturdays, we usually have lunch at home, but today we're having lunch in a restaurant.</u>

4 I / usually / go / on the Ferris wheel but this afternoon / I / go / on the merry-go-round

2 Tim / often / run / on the beach
   but / today / he / run / near a castle

5 Natalie / usually / wear / jeans
   but / today / she / wear / a dress

3 they / usually / play / volleyball at the sports centre
   but this evening / they / play / in the park

6 they / often / stay / in a cottage in summer
   but / this summer / they / stay / on a houseboat

4 **Circle the correct words.**

1 On Fridays we **don't watch** / **aren't watching** much TV.
2 My family and I **go** / **are going** sailing every year.
3 Look! The cat **climbs** / **is climbing** up the tree.
4 I can't come to the sports centre now. I **have** / **am having** lunch.
5 My parents **paint** / **are painting** our new flat at the moment.
6 We **don't often go** / **aren't often going** diving on holiday.

5 **Complete the sentences with the present simple and the present continuous. Use these verbs.**

> build   like   not stay   talk   ~~tell~~   visit

1 Natasha often ____tells____ stories about monsters.
2 I _____ to a guard in the museum at the moment.
3 Mum _____ her job. It's very interesting.
4 In winter, they _____ in their cottage by the sea.
5 Dad is in the garden now. He _____ a tree-house.
6 Every year a lot of people _____ the castle.

6 **Complete the sentences with the present simple and the present continuous. Use the verbs in brackets.**

On Thursday afternoon, I (1) ____don't go____ (not go) straight home after school. I always (2) _____ (meet) my friends in the park near our school. We usually (3) _____ (play) football, and sometimes we (4) _____ (ride) our bikes. We (5) _____ (have) a great time! But today it (6) _____, (rain) so we (7) _____ (watch) a film at my house. We (8) _____ (eat) pizza, and we (9) _____ (have) fun. My sister (10) _____ (not watch) it with us because she (11) _____ (do) her homework!

7 **Say it!** Talk to your partner about what you usually do at the weekend and what you are doing today.

> On Saturday morning, I usually have breakfast in the kitchen, but today I'm having breakfast in the garden.

73

Lesson 2

1 Read.

We must be quiet in the library.

Must

We use **must** to talk about
- what we have to do.
  I **must** go to the dentist.
- what we are obliged to do.
  I **must** do my homework.

Must is followed by the bare infinitive.
We use **must** for the present and the future.
I **must** go home, it's very late.
We **must** study for the test this weekend.

We use **mustn't** to talk about things we are not allowed to do.
You **mustn't** talk to the pilot.

> **Remember!**
>
> It's not very polite to use **must** when we talk to someone we don't know well or to someone older than us.

Affirmative	Negative	Question	Short answers	
I must wash	I mustn't wash	Must I wash …?	Yes, I must.	No, I mustn't.
you must wash	you mustn't wash	Must you wash …?	Yes, you must.	No, you mustn't.
he must wash	he mustn't wash	Must he wash …?	Yes, he must.	No, he mustn't.
she must wash	she mustn't wash	Must she wash …?	Yes, she must.	No, she mustn't.
it must wash	it mustn't wash	Must it wash …?	Yes, it must.	No, it mustn't.
we must wash	we mustn't wash	Must we wash …?	Yes, we must.	No, we mustn't.
you must wash	you mustn't wash	Must you wash …?	Yes, you must.	No, you mustn't.
they must wash	they mustn't wash	Must they wash …?	Yes, they must.	No, they mustn't.

2 **Look at the pictures and complete the sentences with *must* or *mustn't*.**

1 You ____must____ kick the ball.
  You ____mustn't____ touch the ball with your hands.

3 They _____ wear a white shirt to school. Girls _____ wear grey skirts.

2 You _____ eat a lot of junk food.
  You _____ eat more fruit.

4 He _____ pay attention. He _____ fall asleep in school.

3 **Choose the correct answers.**

1 'Must I do my homework?' '____'
  a Yes, you must.
  b No, you mustn't.

2 ____ eat in the museum.
  a Visitors must
  b Visitors mustn't

3 Dad's car doesn't work. ____ fix it?
  a He must
  b Must he

4 My skates are very dirty! ____ clean them for the competition?
  a Must I
  b I must

5 Sally has a test tomorrow. ____ study.
  a She must
  b She mustn't

6 ____ be quiet. The baby is sleeping.
  a We must
  b We mustn't

7 This laptop is very expensive. ____ use it.
  a Mustn't children
  b Children mustn't

8 'Must I go to school?' '____'
  a Yes, you must.
  b No, you mustn't.

4 Look at the pictures about what basketball players must and mustn't do. Write questions and short answers with *must* and *mustn't*.

1. eat a lot of vegetables
<u>Must they eat a lot of vegetables?</u>
<u>Yes, they must.</u>

4. practise every day
_____
_____

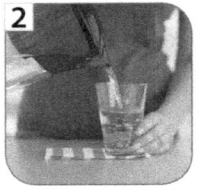
2. drink lots of water
_____
_____

5. go to bed late
_____
_____

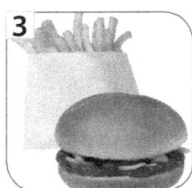
3. eat junk food
_____
_____

6. watch TV all day
_____
_____

5 Complete the telephone conversation using *must* or *mustn't* and these verbs.

> buy   clean   ~~do~~   eat   play   take

Mum: Laura, it's Mum.
Laura: Hi, Mum!
Mum: Laura, we're staying with Uncle Pedro one more night. There are a few things you (1) ____**must do**____ for me.
Laura: OK, Mum.
Mum: First, you (2) _____ some cat food for Flopsy.
Laura: OK. (3) _____ I also _____ the dog for a walk?
Mum: No, your brother can do that, but first, he (4) _____ his room. Oh, and you (5) _____ loud music late at night.
Laura: Ok, Mum. Bye.
Mum: Bye. Oh, and you (6) _____ all the chocolate!

6 Say it! Talk to your partner about what you must or mustn't do at school. Use these suggestions to help you.

- be early for the lesson
- be friendly to our classmates
- clean the classroom
- eat in class
- listen to our teacher
- play jokes on the teacher
- sleep in class
- write on the desks

> We mustn't use mobile phones in class.

76 UNIT 8

Review

1 **Circle the correct words.**

1 Armando **is** / **are** drinking cold water.

2 He **isn't** / **aren't** lying on his bed at the moment.

3 **You're** / **Are you** using a phone in my lesson?

4 We **is** / **are** making a fire to cook lunch.

5 Roberto and I **am not** / **aren't** hiding behind the tree.

6 **They're** / **Are they** looking for the fast food restaurant?

2 **Complete the sentences with the present continuous. Use the verbs in brackets.**

1 Rick _____is using_____ my laptop. (use)

2 Susie _____ for the race! (practise)

3 Lucas and Fernando _____ on the beach. (walk)

4 Shh! I _____ to sleep. (try)

5 We _____ the doors at the moment. (paint)

6 You _____ a great job! (do)

3 **Write sentences with the present continuous.**

1 the boys / not climb / a mountain they / climb / a tree
   The boys aren't climbing a mountain.
   They're/They are climbing a tree.

2 the children / not dance / on the beach they / dance / at the parade
   _____
   _____

3 I / not buy / a salad I / buy / a burger
   _____
   _____

4 Coach Stevens / not smile / at the players he / shout / at them
   _____
   _____

5 Paula and Amanda / not cycle / on the road they / cycle / in the park
   _____
   _____

6 Dad / not fix / his car he / fix / Abdul's kite
   _____
   _____

4 Complete the sentences with *must* or *mustn't*.

1 It's eleven o'clock at night. We __musn't__ play loud music.
2 You _____ wake up your baby sister. She's asleep.
3 I need a book for my science project. I _____ go to the library.
4 She's an athlete. She _____ eat lots of junk food.
5 Very young children _____ use mobile phones.
6 He wants to win the skating competition. He _____ practise every day.

5 Complete the questions with the present continuous using the verbs in brackets. Then complete the short answers.

1 __Is the girl wearing__ a helmet? (the girl / wear)
Yes, __she is__ .

2 _____ pizza? (you / eat)
No, _____ .

3 _____ volleyball? (Mike and Shannon / play)
Yes, _____ .

4 _____ a picture? (John / draw)
No, _____ .

5 _____ to the club today? (you / walk)
Yes, _____ .

6 _____ the winter holiday at home this year? (we / spend)
No, _____ .

6 Complete the sentences with the present continuous. Use these verbs.

| ~~buy~~ go make paint sing spend take |

1 On Monday, Mum __is buying__ me a costume for the carnival.
2 On Tuesday, Dad _____ me to the cinema.
3 On Wednesday, Sara and I _____ in the contest.
4 On Thursday, Mum _____ a chocolate cake.
5 On Friday, I _____ sailing with Uncle Max.
6 On Saturday, Mum and Dad _____ my room.
7 On Sunday, Mum, Dad and I _____ the day at the carnival.

7 Choose the correct answers.

1 I _____ much chocolate.
   a don't usually eat
   b am not usually eating

2 We _____ to Africa by plane at the moment.
   a travel
   b are travelling

3 They _____ early on Sundays.
   a don't always wake up
   b aren't always waking up

4 Mum _____ us a big breakfast at the weekend.
   a often cooks
   b is often cooking

5 _____ your bikes now?
   a Do you wash
   b Are you washing

6 Why _____ at us now?
   a does the coach shout
   b is the coach shouting

78 UNITS 7 – 8

8 Complete the dialogue with the present simple or the present continuous. Use these verbs.

> ~~do~~   help   practise   study   take part   wash

Nico: Hi, Ale. How are you?

Ale: I'm fine, thanks. How are you?

Nico: I'm fine, Ale. What (1) _are you doing_ ?

Ale: Oh, I (2) _____ for the cycling race. It's tomorrow.

Nico: That's exciting.

Ale: Yes, it is. My sister and I (3) _____ in the race every year, but this year she can't. She's got a test on Monday, so she (4) _____ at the moment.

Nico: I see. I always (5) _____ Dad on Saturdays. At the moment, we (6) _____ the car.

Ale: Mmm. Hey, come and watch me in the race!

Nico: Yes, that's a great idea! See you tomorrow.

WRITING PROJECT

9 Look at a project about a popular activity. Circle the correct words.

Camping

Camping (1) **is** / **is being** a very popular activity all around the world. People can relax, forget about school and work, and enjoy nature. Many children and adults (2) **go** / **are going** camping every year.

This family (3) **camps** / **is camping** by the river. They (4) **don't sleep** / **aren't sleeping**. They (5) **sit** / **are sitting** around the fire. They (6) **eat** / **are eating**. It's a lovely place, but they (7) **must be** / **mustn't be** careful because the river can be dangerous. They (8) **mustn't sit** / **must sit** too close to the edge.

10 Now it's your turn to write about a popular activity. Find or draw a picture of the activity and write about it.

Lesson 1

1 Read.

My phone was here this morning!

Past simple: Be

The **past simple** of the verb **be** is **was** and **were**. We use the **past simple** for events, situations and habits in the past.
*The party **was** great fun.*
*The children **were** very quiet.*

In the negative form, we add the word **not** after **was** or **were**. We usually use the short form (**n't**).
*Mandy **wasn't** at school.*
*The boys **weren't** scared.*

In the question form, we use **was** or **were**.
***Was** the train ride interesting?*
***Were** the camels in the desert?*

Time expressions
We often use the following time expressions with the **past simple**. They go at the end or at the beginning of a sentence: **yesterday, yesterday morning/afternoon, last night/week/month/year, two hours/days/weeks ago**, etc.
*I **was** at home **last night**.*
***Last month**, Mum and Dad **were** on holiday.*

Affirmative	Negative	Question	Short answers	
I was	I wasn't (was not)	Was I ...?	Yes, I was.	No, I wasn't.
you were	you weren't (were not)	Were you ...?	Yes, you were.	No, you weren't.
he was	he wasn't (was not)	Was he ...?	Yes, he was.	No, he wasn't.
she was	she wasn't (was not)	Was she ...?	Yes, she was.	No, she wasn't.
it was	it wasn't (was not)	Was it ...?	Yes, it was.	No, it wasn't.
we were	we weren't (were not)	Were we ...?	Yes, we were.	No, we weren't.
you were	you weren't (were not)	Were you ...?	Yes, you were.	No, you weren't.
they were	they weren't (were not)	Were they ...?	Yes, they were.	No, they weren't.

2 Complete the sentences with *was* or *were*.

1 The village _____was_____ beautiful.
2 There _____ lots of people at summer camp.
3 The pizza _____ delicious.
4 The shirt _____ in Mum's suitcase.
5 We _____ in the tent last night.
6 Joaquin _____ in front of the pyramids.
7 Our passports _____ on the table.
8 I _____ at the beach last Saturday.

3 Make the sentences negative.

1 The skiing holiday was fun.   _The skiing holiday wasn't fun._
2 The girls were scared of the spiders.   _____
3 The race was exciting.   _____
4 I was very hungry this morning.   _____
5 Mel and Kim were in India a month ago.   _____
6 We were in Japan last week.   _____

4 Complete the questions with *was* or *were*. Then write short answers.

1 __Was__ the sun cream in the suitcase? ✓
Yes, it was.

2 _____ the old buildings in the city centre? ✗
_____

3 _____ the music too loud? ✓
_____

4 _____ you at the Eiffel Tower yesterday? ✗
_____

5 _____ the rucksacks cheap? ✗
_____

6 _____ Mary in Australia last month? ✓
_____

7 _____ I the winner? ✗
_____

8 _____ your teacher on the train? ✗
_____

There was and There were

The past simple of **there is** and **there are** is **there was** and **there were**. We use **there was** and **there were** to talk or ask about something that existed in the past.
There was *a lot of food on the table.*
There were *three spiders in the tent.*

Affirmative	Negative	Question	Short answers	
There was	There wasn't (There was not)	Was there …?	Yes, there was.	No, there wasn't.
There were	There weren't (There were not)	Were there …?	Yes, there were.	No, there weren't.

5 Complete the sentences with *There was, There were, There wasn't* or *There weren't*.

1 __There were__ many tourists on the beach. ✓
2 _____ much snow on the mountain. ✗
3 _____ any umbrellas in the sand. ✗
4 _____ many people on the plane. ✓
5 _____ a sailing boat in the sea. ✓
6 _____ two swimming pools at the hotel. ✓

6 Circle the correct words.

1 Mum and Dad **wasn't / weren't** on the houseboat last weekend.
2 **Was / Were** the hotel expensive?
3 There **was / were** a lot of people at the parade.
4 **There were / Were there** any snakes in the desert?
5 My trainers **was / were** under the suitcase!
6 Sally **was / were** in France last week.

7 Look at the picture and complete the text with *was, wasn't, were* or *weren't*.

Last month, we (1) __were__ on a boat. It (2) _____ the middle of summer, but it (3) _____ hot. There (4) _____ lots of clouds in the sky. The boat (5) _____ nice, but we (6) _____ very happy because there (7) _____ any seats. It (8) _____ a terrible boat trip!

8 Say it! Think about your holiday last year. Ask and answer these questions with your partner.

- Was it a summer or a winter holiday?
- Were you with your family?
- Were your friends with you?
- Were you at the beach, in the mountains or in the desert?
- Was it boring or interesting?

It was a summer holiday.

We were in the mountains.

Lesson 2

1 Read.

Emi and her family travelled to Athens last summer. They visited the Acropolis and some museums.

Past simple affirmative: Regular verbs

We use the **past simple** for
- actions or situations which started and finished in the past.
  We **stayed** in a hotel on the beach.
- past habits.
  Mum and Dad **travelled** a lot.
- actions which happened one after the other in the past.
  He **washed** his face, **brushed** his teeth and **walked** down the stairs.

We form the affirmative of regular verbs by adding the **–ed** ending.
want   want**ed**

Affirmative
I watched
you watched
he watched
she watched
it watched
we watched
you watched
they watched

When the verb ends in **–e**, we just add **–d**.
use   use**d**

When the verb ends in a consonant + **–y**, we take off the **–y** and add **–ied**.
try   tr**ied**

When the verb ends in a vowel + **–y**, we just add **–ed**.
stay   stay**ed**

When the verb ends in a vowel + consonant, we double the last consonant and add **–ed**.
fit   fit**ted**

When the verb ends in **–l**, we double the **–l** and add **–ed**.
travel   travel**led**

Time expressions
The following time expressions are used with the **past simple**: **yesterday, last night/week/month/year**, etc.
They **travelled** to Japan last year.

Ago
We use **ago** to talk about something that happened a number of years, minutes, days, etc. in the past.
I **arrived ten minutes ago**.
She **visited** Egypt **three years ago**.

2 Complete the tables.

Verb	Past simple
carry	carried
chase	
cry	
fit	
look	

Verb	Past simple
stay	
tie	
travel	
try	
want	

3 Complete the sentences with the past simple. Use the verbs in brackets.

1 The children ____played____ a game after dinner. (play)
2 Amanda's new jeans _____ her well. (fit)
3 The flight _____ at six o'clock. (land)
4 I _____ in a flat near the River Thames. (live)
5 The passengers _____ their tickets and passports. (need)
6 John _____ the bags into the house. (carry)
7 Paul _____ the book about lizards. (like)
8 Susan _____ her T-shirt. (wash)

4 Complete the text with the past simple. Use these verbs.

arrive   ~~decide~~   enjoy   stay   travel   try   visit

Last summer, we (1) ____decided____ to visit our cousins in Alexandria, Egypt. We (2) _____ there by plane. It was a long flight and I was happy when the plane finally (3) _____.

Alexandria is a great place. We (4) _____ at our cousins' house in the city centre for one week. On Monday, we (5) _____ the Bibliotheca Alexandrina. It's an amazing library and it's very, very big!

On Friday night, I (6) _____ Egyptian food in a restaurant. It was delicious! There were lots of people and the music was very good. I (7) _____ my holiday very much.

84 UNIT 9

5 Look at the pictures and complete the sentences with the past simple. Use these verbs.

| brush | climb | cook | count | open | try | wait | watch |

1 Susie ___tried___ the apple juice.

5 My cat _____ up the tree.

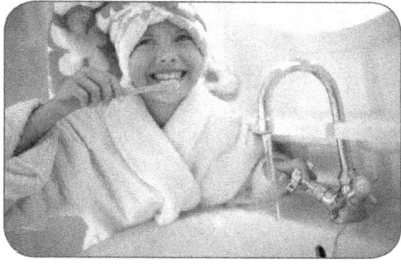

2 Ana _____ her teeth after her bath.

6 Rick _____ all his presents after the party.

3 We _____ the planes at the airport.

7 Ken _____ his coins.

4 Mandy _____ at the bus stop this afternoon.

8 My mum _____ spaghetti for dinner last night.

6 Say it! Talk to your partner about these things.

I played a game last night.

I talked to my best friend last night.

- something you watched on TV
- a game you played
- a person you talked to
- somewhere you visited
- a film you enjoyed

Lesson 3

1 Read.

She bought holiday souvenirs for all her friends.

Past simple affirmative: Irregular verbs

There are lots of irregular verbs in English. Irregular verbs do not follow the rules on page 83. We form the past simple of irregular verbs in different ways. See the Irregular verbs list on page 115.
They **went** on holiday to Singapore.
He **forgot** his passport.

2 Complete the tables.

Verb	Past simple
bring	brought
catch	
come	
fall	
feel	
give	
hold	
keep	

Verb	Past simple
know	knew
put	
ride	
run	
sell	
think	
throw	
win	

3 Complete the sentences with the past simple. Use the verbs in brackets.

1 We _____found_____ a beautiful shell in the sand. (find)
2 Mum and Dad _____ a new tent for our camping trip. (buy)
3 I _____ lots of delicious pizza in Rome. (eat)
4 Cindy _____ a photo of the diving champion! (take)
5 They _____ many tall buildings in New York. (see)
6 Oh no! I _____ my sun cream at home. (leave)
7 You _____ a beautiful dress to the party. (wear)
8 Johnny _____ a wonderful time in Portugal. (have)

4 Look at the pictures and complete the sentences with the past simple. Use these verbs.

| break   cut   ~~draw~~   fall   leave   read |

1 Georgina _____drew_____ a beautiful picture.

4 Veronica _____ her birthday cake.

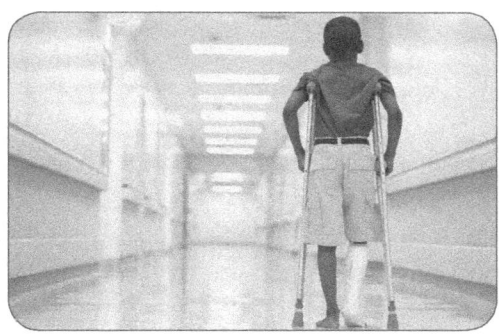

2 Steven _____ his leg on holiday.

5 The ship _____ the port two hours ago.

3 I _____ a really interesting book yesterday.

6 She _____ off her bike.

5 Complete the text with the past simple. Use these verbs.

> be   be   build   eat   ~~fly~~   get   go   go   leave   meet   see

What a wonderful holiday week! We (1) ___flew___ to Barcelona on Saturday morning. The food on the aeroplane (2) _____ great. We (3) _____ to our hotel and (4) _____ our suitcases there. It (5) _____ time to explore! Over the next five days, we (6) _____ amazing places, like Park Güell, Casa Mila and Casa Batlló. Antoni Gaudí (7) _____ all three. We also (8) _____ to many amazing museums. We (9) _____ excellent food at Mercat de la Boqueria, Barcelona's most famous market, and we (10) _____ lots of interesting people. We (11) _____ back home two hours ago. I can't wait to visit Barcelona again!

6 Say it! Talk to your partner about a holiday you enjoyed. Say where you went, who you went with, how you travelled there and what you did there.

> I went to the sea in July. My family and I travelled by aeroplane.

> I went to the mountains in December. I went skiing with my family.

88 UNIT 9

Lesson 1

10

1 Read.

Past simple negative and questions: Regular and irregular verbs

In the negative form, we use **did**, the word **not** and the bare infinitive.
She **didn't go** to the film studio.
We **didn't enjoy** the concert.

In the question form, we use **did** and the bare infinitive.
Did you **get** his autograph?
Did they **give** her the role?

In short answers, we use **did** or **didn't**. We don't use the main verb.
Did Alan buy a puzzle?
Yes, he **did**.
Did Lyn and Caroline go to the party?
No, they **didn't**.

Negative	Question	Short answers	
I didn't come (I did not come)	Did I come ...?	Yes, I did.	No, I didn't.
you didn't come (you did not come)	Did you come ...?	Yes, you did.	No, you didn't.
he didn't come (he did not come)	Did he come ...?	Yes, he did.	No, he didn't.
she didn't come (she did not come)	Did she come ...?	Yes, she did.	No, she didn't.
it didn't come (it did not come)	Did it come ...?	Yes, it did.	No, it didn't.
we didn't come (we did not come)	Did we come ...?	Yes, we did.	No, we didn't.
you didn't come (you did not come)	Did you come ...?	Yes, you did.	No, you didn't.
they didn't come (they did not come)	Did they come ...?	Yes, they did.	No, they didn't.

2 Complete the sentences with the negative form of the past simple. Use the verbs in bold.

1 I **got** the singer's autograph, but I ___didn't get___ the actor's.
2 Mary **saw** the film, but she _____ the play.
3 Max and Sam **went** to the amusement park, but they _____ to the cinema.
4 Melina and I **bought** some burgers, but we _____ any chips.
5 Mark **liked** the songs, but he _____ the books.
6 The cat **played** with the mouse, but it _____ with the ball.

3 Make the sentences negative.

1 The actor wore make-up.
   The actor didn't wear make-up.
2 The audience enjoyed the concert.
   _____
3 He went for an interview.
   _____
4 We found the film studio.
   _____
5 They agreed to shoot a film.
   _____
6 I went on the stage.
   _____

4 Change the sentences into questions.

1 You met a famous scientist.
   Did you meet a famous scientist?
2 They talked to the dancer.
   _____
3 You travelled by boat.
   _____
4 She took part in the competition.
   _____
5 We forgot the tickets.
   _____
6 The pop group sang their most famous song.
   _____

5 Look at the pictures and complete the questions using these verbs. Then write short answers.

climb   ~~meet~~   play   travel   walk   watch

1 ___Did___ Sam ___meet___ a famous tennis player?
   ___Yes, he did.___

2 _____ Dina _____ the guitar at the concert?
   _____

3 _____ the family _____ by aeroplane?
   _____

4 _____ the children _____ TV?
   _____

5 _____ Paul _____ the mountain?
   _____

6 _____ you _____ to school?
   _____

6 Say it! Ask and answer questions with your partner about what you did and didn't do last week. Use these suggestions to help you.

Did you go to the park?

Yes, I did.

- go to the theatre
- see a film
- play video games
- listen to music
- go to a concert
- get a famous person's autograph
- take photos
- have a test

Lesson 2

1 Read.

How did you get up there!?

Question words with the past simple

We use question words with the **past simple** to find out more information about an action in the past.
Who broke the glass? (Jane broke the glass.)
What did Jane **break**? (Jane broke a glass.)
When did Jane **break** the glass? (She broke it yesterday.)
Where did Jane **break** it? (She broke it in her bedroom.)
Which glass **did** she **break**? (She broke the blue one.)
Whose glass **was** it? (It was her mum's.)
Why did she **break** the glass?
(Because she wasn't paying attention.)
How did she **break** it? (She dropped it.)

Remember!

The word order is different in subject and object questions.
Who bought a toy?
(**Mandy** bought a toy.)
What did Mandy **buy**?
(Mandy bought **a toy**.)

2 Circle the correct words.

1 Where **they shot** / **did they shoot** the film?

2 Whose story **the children enjoyed** / **did the children enjoy**?

3 How **you found** / **did you find** tickets to the new musical?

4 Who **thought** / **did they think** the adventure film was exciting?

5 When **she started** / **did she start** acting?

6 Whose bike **rode Jane** / **did Jane ride**?

7 Why **he ate** / **did he eat** your sandwich?

8 Who **you saw** / **did you see** the play with?

3 **Write questions with the past simple.**

1 who / they / give / the award to
  Who did they give the award to?

2 which / actor / Thomas / speak to
  _____

3 who / he / sell / the company to
  _____

4 how / I / lose / my laptop
  _____

5 where / Jake / see a tiger
  _____

6 which medal / the champion / win
  _____

7 why / the cameraman / shout
  _____

8 when / you / have / a riding lesson
  _____

4 **Write questions with the past simple about the underlined words. Use these question words.**

> how   what   when   ~~where~~   who   why

1 Where did you go last summer?
  Last summer I went to Cinque Terre in Italy.

2 _____
  I went there because my grandpa was born in Manarola, a town in Cinque Terre.

3 _____
  I travelled there by train.

4 _____
  I went in July.

5 _____
  I went with Mum, Dad and Grandpa.

6 _____
  We ate delicious local food.

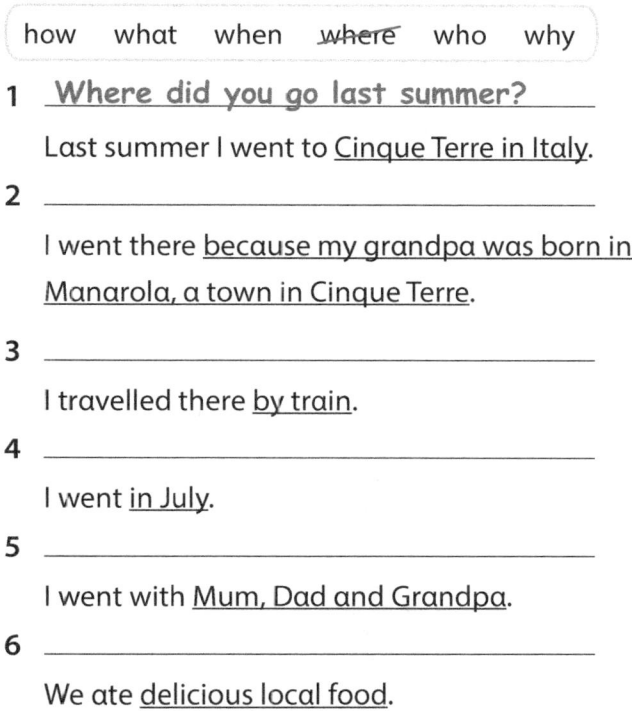

5 **Say it! Imagine that you went somewhere and you met a famous person. Ask and answer questions about this person with your partner. Use these suggestions to help you.**

- Who did you meet?
- When did you meet him or her?
- Where did you meet him or her?
- Why did you go there?
- How did you get there?
- What did he or she say to you?

Who did you meet?

I met Justin Timberlake.

93

Review

1 Choose the correct answers.

1 The western film _____ very exciting.
   - (a) was
   - b were

2 The children _____ from Japan.
   - a wasn't
   - b weren't

3 My flight _____ long.
   - a was
   - b were

4 I _____ at the film studio yesterday.
   - a wasn't
   - b weren't

5 Hana _____ late for school this morning.
   - a was
   - b were

6 We _____ at the hotel last night.
   - a wasn't
   - b weren't

2 Look at the pictures and complete the sentences with *There was*, *There were*, *There wasn't* or *There weren't*.

___There was___ lots of snow last winter.

_____ lots of clothes in the suitcase.

_____ many cruise ships in the port.

_____ two women at the bus stop.

_____ any trees in the desert.

_____ any money in the wallet.

3 Complete the sentences with the past simple. Use the verbs in brackets.

1 Two years ago we ___stayed___ in a beautiful hotel in London. (stay)

2 I _____ my school bag to school. (carry)

3 Sandra _____ to work by train this morning. (travel)

4 The boys _____ us in the playground. (chase)

5 You're late! The lesson _____ at nine o'clock. (start)

6 My parents and I _____ the Eiffel Tower last year. (visit)

94 UNITS 9 – 10

4 Look at the pictures and write questions using the past simple and the words given. Then write short answers.

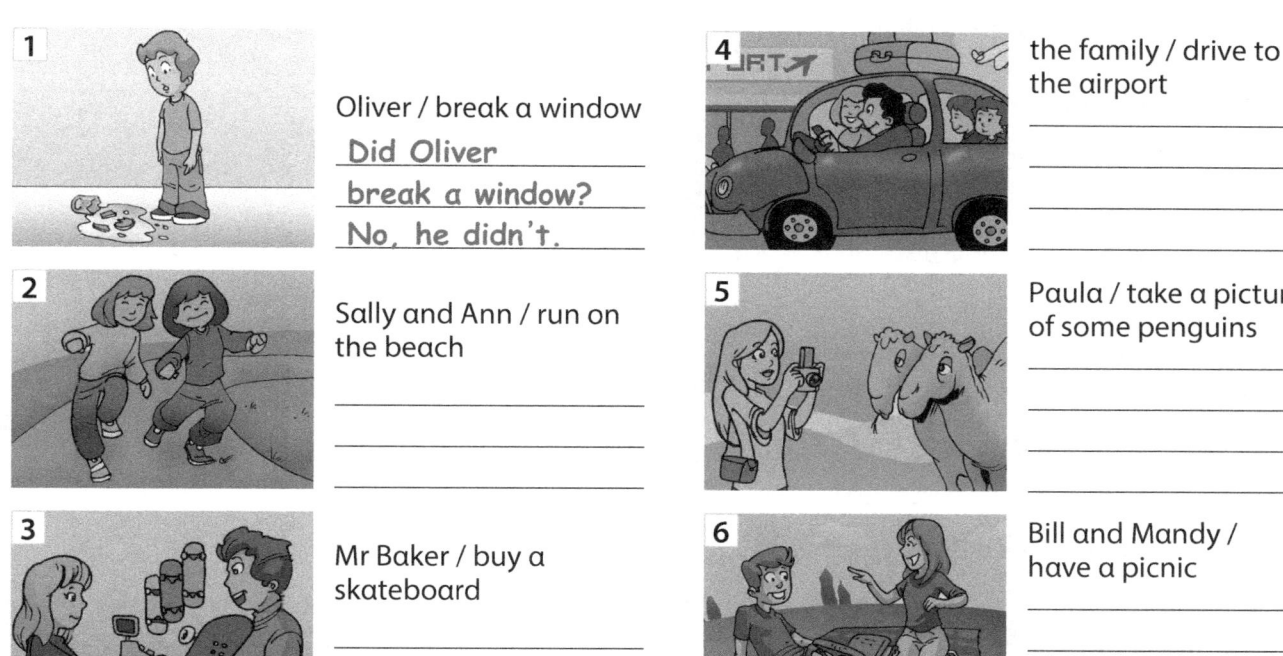

1 Oliver / break a window
   Did Oliver break a window?
   No, he didn't.

2 Sally and Ann / run on the beach
   _____
   _____

3 Mr Baker / buy a skateboard
   _____
   _____

4 the family / drive to the airport
   _____
   _____

5 Paula / take a picture of some penguins
   _____
   _____

6 Bill and Mandy / have a picnic
   _____
   _____

5 Complete the table.

Verb	Past simple
go	went
come	
break	
find	

Verb	Past simple
give	
know	
see	
think	

6 Make the sentences negative. Use the words in brackets.

1 Jill and Mark walked a lot in Paris. (London)
   They/Jill and Mark didn't walk a lot in London.

2 I enjoyed the musical. (film)
   _____

3 Mum took us to the park last week. (theatre)
   _____

4 Steven left his laptop on the plane. (suitcase)
   _____

5 You played tennis yesterday. (basketball)
   _____

6 The cat ate my biscuit! (sandwich)
   _____

7 Write questions with the past simple about the underlined words. Use these question words.

> how   what   ~~when~~   where   who   why

1 <u>When did you go on a cruise?</u>

   I went on a cruise <u>last week</u>.

2 _____

   They visited <u>the pyramids</u>.

3 _____

   I saw <u>my teacher</u> at the airport.

4 _____

   We left our passports <u>at home</u>!

5 _____

   She chose Spanish <u>because she loves Spain</u>.

6 _____

   He travelled to France <u>by train</u>.

WRITING PROJECT

8 Look at a project about a famous person from the past. Complete the project with the past simple of the verbs in brackets.

Tutankhamun

Tutankhamun (1) ___was___ (be) the youngest king of Egypt. He was eight or nine years old when he (2) _____ (become) pharaoh. He was about 19 when he (3) _____ (die).

Howard Carter (4) _____ (discover) Tutankhamun's tomb in 1922. The mummy of the young Egyptian king was inside a beautiful gold coffin. The tomb was amazing. It was full of gold. There (5) _____ (be) also lots of other beautiful things inside.

The pharaohs of Ancient Egypt (6) _____ (want) to take their treasure into the next life, so they (7) _____ (fill) their tombs with beautiful things.

How (8) _____ (Tutankhamun / die)? It is still a mystery.

9 Now it's your turn to do a project about a famous person from the past. Find or draw a picture of the person and write about him or her.

Lesson 1
11

1 Read.

His binoculars are bigger than hers.

Comparatives

We use the **comparative** to compare two people, animals or things. We often use the word **than** after the **comparative**.
*Swans **are bigger than** ducks.*
*A lizard **is smaller than** a crocodile.*

Short adjectives
- We add **–er** to adjectives with one syllable.
  long   long**er**
- When the adjective ends in **–e**, we just add **–r**.
  close   clos**er**
- When the adjective ends in a vowel + consonant, we double the last consonant and add **–er**.
  big   big**ger**
- When the adjective ends in **–y**, we take off the **–y** and add **–ier**.
  dry   dr**ier**

Two-syllable adjectives
- For some two-syllable adjectives (often ending in **–y**, **–le**, **–ow** and **–er**) we can use either **–er** or **more** to form the comparative.
  friendly   friendl**ier** / **more friendly**
  simple   simpl**er** / **more simple**
  narrow   narrow**er** / **more narrow**
  clever   clever**er** / **more clever**
- For adjectives ending in **–y**, adding **–ier** is more common.

Long adjectives
- We form the comparative of long adjectives (two or more syllables) by using the word **more** before the adjective.
  boring   **more boring**
  exciting   **more exciting**

Irregular adjectives
There are irregular adjectives, which do not follow these rules.
good   **better**
bad   **worse**
far   **further/farther**
much/many   **more**
little   **less**

2 Complete the tables.

Adjective	Comparative
big	bigger
fast	
far	
good	
horrible	
hot	
interesting	
pretty	
serious	

Adjective	Comparative
amazing	more amazing
bad	
beautiful	
boring	
close	
dangerous	
exciting	
hard	
long	

3 Complete the sentences with the comparative form of the adjectives in brackets.

1 Egypt is ___hotter___ than England. (hot)
2 Paul is _____ than his brother. (lazy)
3 My binoculars are _____ than Teddy's. (expensive)
4 The road is _____ than the path. (wide)
5 The orange butterfly is _____ than the blue one. (small)
6 Kathy's science mark is _____ than mine. (bad)
7 Simon is _____ than Henry. (intelligent)
8 Kate's hair is _____ than mine. (short)

4 Complete the sentences with the comparative form of these adjectives.

~~cheap~~   cold   good   heavy   small

1 The small torch is __cheaper__ than the big torch.
2 The fish on the right is _____ than the one on the left.
3 The elephant is _____ than the chimp.

4 John's drawing is _____ than Paul's.
5 The penguin's home is _____ than the lion's.

as ... as

We can also use **as** + adjective + **as** to compare two people, animals or things. We use **as ... as** when the two people, animals or things are the same.
*Sally is **as sweet as** Julie.*

We use **not as** + adjective + **as** when the two people, animals or things aren't the same.
*The dolphin is**n't as big as** the whale.*

5 Complete the sentences. Use *as ... as* and *not as ... as*.

1 Oliver is _____as old as_____ Tiger. (old)
2 Oliver is _____ Tiger. (heavy)
3 Tiger is _____ Oliver. (loud)
4 Oliver is _____ Tiger. (friendly)
5 Oliver is _____ Tiger. (hungry)

6 Say it! Use the comparative form to talk about pets with your partner. Use these suggestions to help you.

- cat
- dog
- mouse
- spider
- rabbit
- lizard

- friendly
- good
- horrible
- nice
- sweet
- tiny

Cats are nicer than dogs.

Cats are friendlier than rabbits.

Lesson 2

1 Read.

My hamster is the best pet in the world!

Superlatives

We use the **superlative** to compare more than two people, animals or things. We use the word **the** before the superlative. We often use a phrase with *in* or *of* to continue the sentence.
*My kitten is **the cutest** of all.*
*The cheetah is **the fastest** animal in the world.*

Short adjectives
- We add **–est** to adjectives with one syllable.
  cold   the cold**est**
- When the adjective ends in –**e**, we just add –**st**.
  nice   the nice**st**
- When the adjective ends in a vowel + consonant, we double the last consonant and add –**est**.
  big   the bigg**est**
- When the adjective ends in –**y**, we take off the –**y** and add –**iest**.
  dry   the dr**iest**

Two-syllable adjectives
- For some two-syllable adjectives (often ending in –**y**, –**le**, –**ow** and –**er**), we can use either –**est** or **the most** to form the superlative.
  friendly   the friendl**iest** / the most friendly
  simple   the simpl**est** / the most simple
  narrow   the narrow**est** / the most narrow
  clever   the clever**est** / the most clever
- For adjectives ending in –**y**, adding –**est** is more common.

Long adjectives
- We form the superlative of long adjectives (two or more syllables) by using the words **the most** before the adjective.
  boring   **the most boring**
  important   **the most important**

Irregular adjectives
There are irregular adjectives, which do not follow these rules.
good   **the best**
bad   **the worst**
far   **the furthest / the farthest**
much/many   **the most**
little   **the least**

2 Complete the table.

Adjective	Comparative	Superlative
bad	worse	the worst
difficult	more difficult	
easy	easier	
good	better	
hard	harder	
hot	hotter	
important	more important	
many	more	
popular	more popular	
strange	stranger	

3 Complete the sentences with the superlative form of the adjectives in brackets.

1 My puppy is ___the noisiest___ pet in the neighbourhood! (noisy)
2 Helen's pony is _____ of all! (fast)
3 I went to _____ carnival last week. (boring)
4 We saw _____ eagle. (amazing)
5 The goldfish was _____ fish in the bowl. (small)
6 James is _____ boy in our class. He's got a pet parrot! (lucky)

4 Complete the dialogue with the superlative form of the adjectives in brackets.

Richie: Hi, Maggie. Did you enjoy your birthday party?

Maggie: Yes, I did.

Richie: It was (1) ___the best___ (good) party this year.

Maggie: Yes, it was. The clowns were wonderful. Max was (2) _____ (funny) clown.

Richie: Yes, he was and we played some great games. The food was nice, too. I loved the burgers and pizza, but the cake was (3) _____ (tasty).

Maggie: Mum and Dad got me (4) _____ (unusual) present.

Richie: What did they get you?

Maggie: A parrot. It says (5) _____ (silly) things and it's got (6) _____ (beautiful) colours.

Richie: Oh, parrots are my favourite pets!

5 Look at the pictures and complete the sentences with the superlative form of these adjectives.

> big   lazy   ~~long~~   many   small   slow

1 The monkey has got __the longest__ tail.

4 Africa has got _____ elephants in the world.

2 The white cat is _____ cat. It wakes up at eight o'clock!

5 The dinosaur's egg is _____ .

3 The tortoise is _____ animal in the race.

6 Tim's dog is _____ !

6 Say it! Use the superlative form to talk about some of your favourite things and animals with your partner. Use these suggestions to help you.

> Cats are the best pets.

> No, rabbits are the best pets.

- good / film
- interesting / book
- cute / pet

- big / pet
- tall / animal
- good / song

Lesson 3

1 Read.

Mariela is older than Marco.
Antonio is the oldest of the three.

Marco   Antonio   Mariela

Comparatives and superlatives

We use the **comparative** to compare two people, animals or things. We use the **superlative** to compare more than two people, animals or things. In a **superlative** sentence, we compare one person, animal or thing to a group of people, animals or things.

Rabbits are **popular** pets.

Hamsters are **more popular than** rabbits.

Cats are **the most popular** pet.

Hippos are **big**.

Elephants are **bigger than** hippos.

The blue whale is **the biggest** animal in the world.

There are **many** animals on our farm.

There are **more** animals on my uncle's farm **than** on our farm.

My grandpa's farm has **the most** animals.

as ... as

We can also use **as** + adjective + **as** to compare two people, animals or things. We use **as ... as** when the two people, animals or things are the same. We use **not as ... as** when the two people, animals or things are not the same.

My cat is not **as big as** your cat.
My brother is **not as tall as** me.

Remember!

See the rules for comparative and superlative forms on pages 97 and 100.

2 Circle the correct words.

1 Erica's dog is **friendlier** / **the friendliest** than Sam's.
2 Peter's house is **bigger than** / **the biggest** in the street.
3 I have got **most** / **more** books than you.
4 Carla is **tall** / **taller** than her brother.
5 The maths test was **easier** / **the easiest** than the geography test.
6 Joanne is **the best** / **better than** student in my class.
7 This peacock has got **brighter** / **the brightest** colours than that peacock.
8 Our cat sleeps inside at night because it's **warmer** / **the warmest** than in the garden.

3 Choose the correct answers.

1 Monkeys are _____ worms.
 a the most clever
 b more clever than

2 My binoculars are _____ as the scientist's.
 a as good
 b better than

3 The zoo is _____ the park.
 a the furthest
 b further than

4 The cave at the end of the beach is _____ all.
 a scarier than
 b the scariest of

5 Fish is _____ meat.
 a healthier than
 b the healthiest

6 The pirate costume is _____ than the cowboy's.
 a more popular
 b the most popular

7 Chimpanzees are not _____ as lions.
 a more dangerous
 b as dangerous

8 The cat has got _____ food on its plate than the dog.
 a the least
 b less

4 Complete the sentences using the comparative or superlative forms of the adjectives in brackets.

1 My brother is ____taller than____ me, but my sister is ____the tallest____ . (tall)
2 I am _____ most of my friends, but Marla is _____ in our class. (young)
3 Goldfish are popular pets, but I think hamsters are _____ goldfish, and cats are _____ pet. (popular)
4 I think crocodiles are _____ animals in the world! (amazing)
5 Mum's cakes are good, but Grandma makes _____ cakes. (delicious)
6 I think apples are _____ oranges, but strawberries are _____ fruit. (tasty)

104 UNIT 11

5 Complete the text with the comparative or the superlative form of these adjectives.

> delicious   early   ~~good~~   more   near   old   pretty   quick   tired   young

Last Monday was the (1) _____best_____ day of the week! We finished school at one o'clock and we went to a farm. The (2) _____ farm to our school is 16 km away. We went by bus. It was the (3) _____ way to get there.

There were many beautiful animals at the farm. The (4) _____ birds were the peacocks. They were amazing! There were also lots of cows and sheep. I think there were (5) _____ cows than sheep. Some were babies! You can see the (6) _____ cow in the photo. Ana and I are petting it. She was just two months old. There were also two horses. They looked very similar, but one looked (7) _____. Maybe it was the mum!

At five o'clock we sat down on the grass and had a picnic. We were all very hungry and tired. They sold ice cream at the farm, so I bought the (8) _____ chocolate ice cream ever!

By the time we got home, I was (9) _____ than usual, so I went to bed very early, even (10) _____ than my baby sister!

6 Say it! Talk to your partner about your family, friends and school subjects, using the comparative and superlative forms.

> My brother is taller than me.

> My father is the tallest in our family.

105

Lesson 1

1 Read.

It's going to rain.

Be going to

We use **be going to**
- to talk about future plans and intentions.
  I'm going to play in the park this afternoon.
- to predict that something is going to happen, when we have some proof or some information.
  The sky is blue. It**'s going to be** a nice day.

Be going to is followed by the bare infinitive.
We**'re going to visit** our grandparents tonight.

Time expressions
We often use the following time expressions with **be going to**. They go at the beginning or at the end of the sentence: **tonight, tomorrow, soon, later on, in the morning/ evening, this afternoon/ weekend, next week/year, in a week/month,** etc.

Affirmative	Negative
I'm going to buy	I'm not going to buy
you're going to buy	you aren't going to buy
he's going to buy	he isn't going to buy
she's going to buy	she isn't going to buy
it's going to buy	it isn't going to buy
we're going to buy	we aren't going to buy
you're going to buy	you aren't going to buy
they're going to buy	they aren't going to buy

Question	Short answers	
Am I going to buy ...?	Yes, I am.	No, I'm not.
Are you going to buy ...?	Yes, you are.	No, you aren't.
Is he going to buy ...?	Yes, he is.	No, he isn't.
Is she going to buy ...?	Yes, she is.	No, she isn't.
Is it going to buy ...?	Yes, it is.	No, it isn't.
Are we going to buy ...?	Yes, we are.	No, we aren't.
Are you going to buy ...?	Yes, you are.	No, you aren't.
Are they going to buy ...?	Yes, they are.	No, they aren't.

2 Complete the sentences with *be going to*. Use the verbs in brackets.

1 The clouds are very black. It __'s/is going to rain__ . (rain)
2 This weekend we _____ with our grandparents. (stay)
3 My parents _____ me a laptop for my birthday. (get)
4 I can hear footsteps. They _____ us! (find)
5 It's sunny. You _____ a lovely day at the beach. (have)
6 Phillip _____ Egypt in February. (visit)

3 Complete the sentences with the negative form of *be going to*. Use the verbs in brackets.

1 I __'m not going to tidy__ my bedroom tonight. (tidy)
2 My sister _____ to the party. She wasn't invited. (go)
3 This puzzle is very difficult. We _____ it today. (finish)
4 They're terrible singers! They _____ the contest. (win)
5 Mum _____ me the laptop. It's very expensive. (buy)
6 It's sunny. I _____ my raincoat to school. (wear)

4 Complete the questions using *be going to* and the words in brackets. Then complete the short answers.

1 __Is Max going to take__ an umbrella? (Max / take)
No, _____ .
2 _____ your homework tonight? (you / do)
Yes, _____ .
3 _____ in the cave? (they / sleep)
No, _____ .
4 _____ to the moon? (the astronaut / travel)
Yes, _____ .
5 _____ the invitations this afternoon? (you / send)
No, _____ .

5 Complete the text with *be going to*. Use the verbs in brackets.

Every Saturday, Josh and I play basketball, but tomorrow we (1) __aren't going to play__ (not play). Mum and Dad (2) _____ (take) us to the mountains because it (3) _____ (snow). I can't wait!
We (4) _____ (wake up) at 6.30 in the morning and Dad (5) _____ (drive) us to the mountains. I like travelling by car and I usually fall asleep!
Josh and I (6) _____ (go) skiing. We're not very good, but we like it. Mum and Dad (7) _____ (not try) it. They want to watch us!
It (8) _____ (be) a very exciting day.

6 Look at the pictures and complete the sentences with *be going to*. Use these verbs.

| fly   go   have   play   ~~ride~~   visit |

1 On Monday, I ____'m/am going____
   ____to ride____ my bike.

2 On Tuesday, Dad and I _____
   _____ a kite.

3 On Wednesday, I _____
   _____ sailing with Dad and
   Andy.

4 On Thursday, we _____
   _____ football.

5 On Friday, we _____
   _____ a picnic in the park.

6 On Saturday, we _____
   _____ our grandparents in
   the countryside.

7 Say it! Talk to your partner about what you are going to do this summer. Use these suggestions to help you.

> I'm going to visit my cousins in Sydney.

> Wow! I'm going to learn Japanese.

- trips / journeys / holidays
- outdoor activities
- entertainment
- unusual plans

108   UNIT 12

Lesson 2

1 Read.

Hold my hand. I'll help you.

Future simple

We use the **future simple**
- to predict the future.
  *People **will live** on other planets one day.*
- for decisions we make at the time of speaking.
  *We**'ll come** for a walk, too.*
- for offers, promises, threats and warnings.
  *I**'ll take** you for a swim, I promise.*
- to ask somebody to do something for us.
  ***Will** you **walk** to the beach with me, please?*
- after phrases such as **I think**, **I'm sure**, **I hope**, **I bet**, etc.
  *I'm sure we**'ll save** the rainforest.*

We form the affirmative with **will** and the bare infinitive.
*Cathy and I **will buy** the presents.*

We form the negative with **will**, the word **not** and the bare infinitive. We usually use the short form (**won't**).
*Stevie **won't help** me with my homework.*

We form questions with **will** and the bare infinitive.
***Will** Alex **come** with us?*

We form short answers with **will** or **won't**. We don't use the main verb.
***Will** you **meet** Paul tonight?*
*Yes, I **will**.*
***Will** it **rain** tomorrow?*
*No, it **won't**.*

Affirmative	Negative
I'll come (will come)	I won't come (will not come)
you'll come (will come)	you won't come (will not come)
he'll come (will come)	he won't come (will not come)
she'll come (will come)	she won't come (will not come)
it'll come (will come)	it won't come (will not come)
we'll come (will come)	we won't come (will not come)
you'll come (will come)	you won't come (will not come)
they'll come (will come)	they won't come (will not come)

Question	Short answers	
Will I come ...?	Yes, I will.	No, I won't.
Will you come ...?	Yes, you will.	No, you won't.
Will he come ...?	Yes, he will.	No, he won't.
Will she come ...?	Yes, she will.	No, she won't.
Will it come ...?	Yes, it will.	No, it won't.
Will we come ...?	Yes, we will.	No, we won't.
Will you come ...?	Yes, you will.	No, you won't.
Will they come ...?	Yes, they will.	No, they won't.

Time expressions
We often use the following time expressions with the **future simple**. They go at the beginning or at the end of a sentence: **tonight, tomorrow, soon, later on, in the morning/evening, this afternoon/weekend, next week/year, in a week/month**, etc.

2 **Match.**

1. It's a lovely morning.
2. I'm going to a party today.
3. Let's take Mum skiing for her birthday.
4. It's really hot.
5. Don't cut down any more trees.
6. I can't do my science homework!

a. I'm sure you'll have a great time.
b. Don't worry, I'll help you with it.
c. John and I will walk to school.
d. She will enjoy it.
e. I think I'll have a cold drink.
f. You'll destroy the park.

3 **Make the sentences negative.**

1. Mum and Dad will put up our tent.
   <u>Mum and Dad won't put up our tent.</u>
2. Uncle Todd will take us to the amusement park.
   _____
3. They'll sleep in the tent.
   _____
4. It'll be foggy tomorrow morning.
   _____
5. Isabel will win the race.
   _____
6. We'll look for information about the canyon.
   _____

4 **Write questions with the future simple. Then complete the short answers.**

1. Amy / talk about / rainforests
   <u>Will Amy talk about rainforests?</u>
   Yes, <u>she will</u>.
2. Juan and Cata / bring / photos / of waterfalls
   _____
   No, _____.
3. Susie and I / talk about / our holiday
   _____
   No, _____.
4. Roberto / give / me / book / about wild animals
   _____
   Yes, _____.
5. Mum / walk / in the forest / with me
   _____
   Yes, _____.
6. you / show us / pictures of the canyon
   _____
   No, _____.

110 UNIT 12

5 Look at the pictures and complete the sentences with the future simple. Use these verbs.

buy ~~carry~~ fly get have swim

1. This picnic basket is very heavy. I __'ll/will carry__ it for you.
2. Do you want some lemonade? No, I _____ any, thanks.
3. Bye, Mum! Don't go out, you _____ wet.
4. What a pretty butterfly! Don't shout. It _____ away.
5. The sea is dirty! You're right. We _____ here.
6. There isn't any juice, Mum. I _____ some from the supermarket.

6 Say it! Talk with your partner about what you will do to help protect the environment. Use these suggestions to help you.

I'll use less water when I shower.

That's a good idea. I'll pick up rubbish at the beach.

- clean the streets
- pick up rubbish at the beach
- plant trees

- use less paper / save water
- talk to people about rainforests

Review

1 Complete the sentences with the comparative form of the adjectives in brackets.

1 My history mark was _____lower_____ than Sarah's. (low)
2 Your carnival costume is _____ than my costume. (good)
3 Chinese is _____ than French. (difficult)
4 Comics are _____ than books. (exciting)
5 The rain is _____ than it was yesterday. (heavy)
6 The bus stop is _____ than the train station. (far)

2 Complete the sentences with the superlative form of the adjectives in brackets.

1 Volleyball is __the most popular__ sport at our school. (popular)
2 That was _____ cycling race! (good)
3 Yesterday was _____ day of the month. (cloudy)
4 Clare's boots are _____ of all. (expensive)
5 I watched _____ film on Friday night. (scary)
6 Vicky is _____ girl in our school. (tall)

3 Complete the sentences with as ... as and not as ... as and the adjectives in brackets.

1 Dad is 38 years old. Mum is 34 years old.
   Dad is __not as young as__ Mum. (young)
2 In England, it is often cold. In Jordan, it's usually hot.
   England is _____ Jordan. (hot)
3 The museum building is 30 metres tall. The cinema building is also 30 metres tall.
   The museum building is _____ the cinema building. (tall)
4 Fifteen students in my class enjoy science lessons. Twenty-five students enjoy history lessons.
   Science lessons are _____ history lessons. (popular)
5 Helena's suitcase weighs 15 kg. Carla's suitcase also weighs 15 kg.
   Carla's suitcase is _____ Helena's suitcase. (heavy)

4 Complete the sentences with the comparative or superlative form of the adjectives in brackets.

1 Mario is __the youngest__ student in our class. (young)
2 Some video games are _____ some films. (popular)
3 Being a good friend is _____ thing. (important)
4 I'm _____ my sister, but my brother is _____ in the family. (tall)
5 Cats are good pets, but hamsters are _____ pets. (good)

5 Complete the sentences with the future simple. Use the verbs in brackets.

1 I _____'ll/will give_____ you your medicine. (give)
2 I promise we _____ a trick on you. (not play)
3 You can use Dad's laptop. I _____ him. (not tell)
4 There's someone at the front door. _____ it? (you / open)
5 _____ the houseboat? (they / sell)
6 _____ lost? (we / get)
7 Dad _____ you to the airport. (drive)
8 The skiing holiday _____ great! (be)

6 Look at the pictures and complete the questions using *be going to* and the words in brackets. Then write short answers.

1 __Is Luke going to win__ the race? (Luke / win)
   __No, he isn't.__

2 _____ in the library today? (you / study)
   _____

3 _____ a bus? (they / catch)
   _____

4 _____ cold today? (it / be)
   _____

5 _____ a party for her birthday? (Nadia / have)
   _____

6 _____ new trees? (they / plant)
   _____

7 Complete the text with the correct form of *be going to*. Use the verbs in brackets.

Next week, Mum, Dad, Tom and I (1) ___are going to go___ (go) on a walking holiday in the mountains. I often go to the mountains because my cousins live nearby, and we all love walking and cycling.

Dad (2) _____ (not drive) because we (3) _____ (travel) by train. We (4) _____ (stop) at our grandparents' farm for lunch. Grandma and Grandad have got lots of animals!

This year, we (5) _____ (not sleep) at my cousins' house. We (6) _____ (stay) in a lovely hotel, and we (7) _____ (take part) in a long walk with lots of other people. I (8) _____ (not cycle) this time.

We (9) _____ (have) a great time!

WRITING PROJECT

8 Look at a project about the highest mountain in the world. Complete the project with the comparative or superlative form of the adjectives in brackets.

Mount Everest

Mount Everest is (1) ___the highest___ (high) mountain in the world. It is 8,850 m high. It is on the border between Nepal and Tibet. Climbing Mount Everest is (2) _____ (difficult) than climbing most mountains in the world. Many people from all over the world want to climb Mount Everest. They know that it will be (3) _____ (hard) than anything else they do in their lives. They also know that it will be (4) _____ (exciting)!

The (5) _____ (young) person to climb Mount Everest is Jordan Romero. He was 13 years old when he climbed it in 2010. The (6) _____ (old) person to climb Mount Everest is Yuichiro Miura. He climbed it in 2003 when he was 70 years old and again in 2013 when he was 80.

Anyone who climbs Mount Everest will remember it all of their life!

9 Now it's your turn to do a project about the highest mountain or the most interesting place to visit in your country. Find or draw a picture of the mountain or place and write about it.

Irregular verbs

Infinitive	Past simple	Past participle
be	was/were	been
become	became	become
begin	began	begun
bet	bet	bet
bite	bit	bitten
break	broke	broken
bring	brought	brought
build	built	built
burn	burnt	burnt
buy	bought	bought
catch	caught	caught
choose	chose	chosen
come	came	come
cost	cost	cost
cut	cut	cut
die	died	died
dig	dug	dug
do	did	done
draw	drew	drawn
drink	drank	drunk
drive	drove	driven
eat	ate	eaten
fall	fell	fallen
feed	fed	fed
feel	felt	felt
fight	fought	fought
find	found	found
fly	flew	flown
forget	forgot	forgotten
freeze	froze	frozen
get	got	got
give	gave	given
go	went	gone
grow	grew	grown
have	had	had
hear	heard	heard
hide	hid	hidden
hit	hit	hit
hold	held	held
hurt	hurt	hurt
keep	kept	kept

Infinitive	Past simple	Past participle
know	knew	known
learn	learnt	learnt
leave	left	left
lend	lent	lent
let	let	let
lie	lay	lain
lose	lost	lost
make	made	made
mean	meant	meant
meet	met	met
pay	paid	paid
put	put	put
read	read	read
ride	rode	ridden
ring	rang	rung
run	ran	run
say	said	said
see	saw	seen
sell	sold	sold
send	sent	sent
shoot	shot	shot
show	showed	shown
sing	sang	sung
sit	sat	sat
sleep	slept	slept
smell	smelt	smelt
speak	spoke	spoken
spend	spent	spent
stand	stood	stood
steal	stole	stolen
swim	swam	swum
take	took	taken
teach	taught	taught
tell	told	told
think	thought	thought
throw	threw	thrown
understand	understood	understood
wake	woke	woken
wear	wore	worn
win	won	won
write	wrote	written

Notes

Notes

Notes

Notes

Wonderful World 3 Grammar Book, Second Edition

Vice President, Editorial Director: John McHugh
Executive Editor: Eugenia Corbo, Siân Mavor
Commissioning Editor: Kayleigh Buller
Head of Strategic Marketing EMEA ELT: Charlotte Ellis
Product Marketing Executive: Ellen Setterfield
Head of Production and Design: Celia Jones
Senior Content Project Manager: Phillipa Davidson-Blake
Manufacturing Manager: Eyvett Davis
Cover Design: Lisa Trager
Interior Design and Composition: Lumina Datamatics, Inc.

© 2019 National Geographic Learning, a Cengage Learning Company

ALL RIGHTS RESERVED. No part of this work covered by the copyright herein may be reproduced or distributed in any form or by any means, except as permitted by U.S. copyright law, without the prior written permission of the copyright owner.

"National Geographic", "National Geographic Society" and the Yellow Border Design are registered trademarks of the National Geographic Society ® Marcas Registradas

For product information and technology assistance, contact us at
Cengage Learning Customer & Sales Support, cengage.com/contact
For permission to use material from this text or product, submit all requests online at **cengage.com/permissions**
Further permissions questions can be emailed to
permissionrequest@cengage.com

Grammar Book: Level 3
ISBN: 978-1-4737-6082-0

National Geographic Learning
Cheriton House, North Way
Andover, Hampshire, SP10 5BE
United Kingdom

National Geographic Learning, a Cengage Learning Company, has a mission to bring the world to the classroom and the classroom to life. With our English language programs, students learn about their world by experiencing it. Through our partnerships with National Geographic and TED Talks, they develop the language and skills they need to be successful global citizens and leaders.

Locate your local office at **international.cengage.com/region**

Visit National Geographic Learning online at **NGL.Cengage.com/ELT**
Visit our corporate website at **www.cengage.com**

Photo Credits

5(ml) MetaTools; **5(bl)** ImageSource; **50(mr)** Premier Edition Image Library/Superstock; **50(ml)** Ingram Publishing/Superstock; **64(ml)** Corel; **73** Jose Luis Pelaez Inc/Blend Images; **76(tl)** MetaTools; **76(bl)** Artville; **85(tml)** Randy Faris; **91(br)** Opus/a.collectionRF/amanaimages/Corbis; **114(b)** Jagdish Agarwal/Corbis

© Alamy Stock Photo: 4 DigitalVision; **52(ml)** UpperCut Images; **52(bl)** Somos Images; **87(ml)** ERproductions Ltd/Blend Images

© Getty Images: 49(mr) Eyewire/Getty Images; **50(tl)** PhotoDisc; **57(ml)** PLAINVIEW/E+; **66(bl)** PhotoDisc; **84** Holgs/E+; **86** Imgorthand/E+; **91(ml)** Getty Images; **91(mr)** PhotoDisc; **92** Ronnie Kaufman/Larry Hirshowitz/ Blend Images; **108(ml)** PhotoDisc; **114(t)** PhotoDisc

© Image state: 5(mm) JohnFoxxImages; **52(mr)** John Foxx Image

© istockphoto: 5(tm) istockphoto; **49(ml)** Jill Chen; **76(tr)** Razvan Radu

© Jupiterimages: 5(bml) BananaStock/Jupiterimages; **11** BananaStock/Jupiterimages; **29** Comstock/Jupiterimages; **108(br)** BananaStock/Jupiterimages; **110** BrandX/Jupiterimages

© Shutterstock: 5(tl) AndreasGradin; **5(tr)** KristianSekulic; **5(mr)** MilanIlicPhotographer; **5(bmr)** Michaeljung; **5(br)** EmiliaStasiak; **6** Thitisan; **7** BannykhAlexeyVladimirovich; **8(tl)** IvonneWierink; **8(tr)** Vladimir1984; **10** Gorillaimages; **13** Wavebreakmedia; **15** Photographee.eu; **17** AVAVA; **19(tl)** Anna Grigorjeva; **19(ml)** Alena Ozerova; **19(bl)** Lakov Filimonov; **19(tr)** Asia Images Group; **19(mr)** JPC-PROD; **19(br)** Jacek Chabraszewski; **20** Purino; **24(tm)** DibasUA; **24(tr)** TanaCh; **24(bl)** Diego Cervo; **24(bm)** Andrewpotter4; **24(br)** Natchapon L.; **26** Andrea Izzotti; **27** Diego Cervo; **30** Darrin Henry; **33(l)** Pressmaster; **33(r)** Photographee.eu; **36** AVAVA; **39** Soloviova Liudmyla; **44** Galyna Andrushko; **45** Michal Kowalski; **48** Zoriana Zaitseva; **49(tl)** Robyn Mackenzie; **49(bl)** Erika Cross; **49(tr)** Stockyimages; **49(br)** Elnur; **50(tr)** Sosha; **50(br)** Viktor1; **50(bl)** Nata-Lia; **51** Andrey Armyagov; **52(tl)** Dudarev Mikhail; **52(tr)** Racheal Grazias; **52(br)** Connie Lanyon-Roberts; **53** AnastasiaNi; **54** Nd3000; **56** Simone van den Berg; **57(tl)** Michael Pettigrew; **57(bl)** Davydenko Yuliia; **57(tr)** Dudarev Mikhail; **57(mr)** DenisNata; **57(br)** Africa Studio; **61** Reneefairhurst; **62** Juriah Mosin; **64(tl)** Li Jianbing; **64(bl)** Jakub Cejpek; **64(tr)** De Visu; **64(br)** 64(mr); **64(mr)** Michaeljung; **65** Kevin Hellon; **66(tl)** Casezy idea; **66(ml)** Alexei_tm; **66(tr)** Rich Carey; **66(mr)** Boris Mrdja; **66(br)** Purino; **68** PR Image Factory; **69** Hurst Photo; **71** Gladskikh Tatiana; **74** Eakphum; **75(tl)** Fotokostic; **75(bl)** NatashaPhoto; **75(bm)** Stephen B. Goodwin; **75(tr)** Monkey Business Images; **75(br)** Wavebreakmedia; **76(ml)** Alliance; **76(mr)** PaulPaladin **79** Rawpixel.com; **80** Syda Productions; **83** RYUSHI; **85(tl)** Maryna Kulchytska; **85(bml)** Aleksei Potov; **85(bl)** Vietnam Stock Images; **85(tr)** Yiannis Papadimitriou; **85(tmr)** Wavebreakmedia; **85(bmr)** Arapix; **85(br)** Nitr; **87(tl)** Jacek Chabraszewski; **87(bl)** George Rudy; **87(tr)** Rikard Stadler; **87(mr)** Ruth Peterkin; **87(br)** Syaheir Azizan; **88** MarinaDa; **89** Oliveromg; **91(tl)** PROMA1; **91(bl)** Blaz Kure; **91(tr)** Stefano Tinti; **93** Muratart; **94(tl)** Zoran Ras; **94(ml)** Bikeriderlondon; **94(bl)** Elijah Lovkoff; **94(tr)** Carlo Dapino; **94(mr)** Katiekk; **94(br)** KIRATIYA KUMKAEW; **96** Mountainpix; **97** Pavel L Photo and Video; **99** Jeafish Ping; **100** Smit; **101** Anastacia - azzzya; **103** Gino Santa Maria; **104** Wavebreakmedia; **105** Alexkatkov; **106** Waraphorn Aphai; **108(tl)** Wavebreakmedia; **108(tr)** Fotokostic; **108(mr)** Stockcreations; **109** Viacheslav Nikolaenko; **108(bl)** Shutterstock

Printed and bound by CPI Group (UK) Ltd, Croydon, CR0 4YY
Print Number: 06 Print Year: 2025